BLIND RAGE

To Jackie,
I'm so glad to see you
again

BLIND RAGE

A TRUE STORY OF SIN, SEX, AND MURDER IN A SMALL ARKANSAS TOWN

Anita Paddock

by ANITA PADDOCK

August 11, 2015

𝓟
Pen-L Publishing
Fayetteville, Arkansas
Pen-L.com

This book is dedicated to my fellow classmates of the 1958 graduating class of Van Buren High School, those sadly gone from our lives and those still here among us. Thank you for electing me your class president, my first honor, and perhaps my best.

DEFINITION OF BLIND RAGE:

Rage can sometimes lead to a state of mind where the individual is capable of doing things that may normally seem physically impossible. A person in rage may also experience tunnel vision, muffled hearing, increased heart rate, and hyperventilation.
A person in a state of rage may also lose much of the capacity for rational thought and reasoning, and may act violently on impulses until the source of their rage is destroyed.
People in a rage have described experiencing things in slow motion and may suffer a form of amnesia regarding the incident itself.

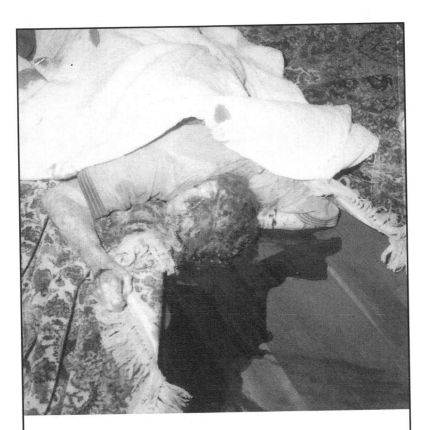

**Crime scene photograph
May 17, 1981**

CHAPTER ONE

MAY 16, 1981

Ruie Ann Park glanced at herself in the bathroom mirror. Her head was covered with thirty pin curls held in place by thirty bobby pins. On her chest were red splotches, sure signs she was angry. She grabbed her pink nylon robe from the hook behind the door and threw it over her matching nightgown with an exaggerated motion that made the robe fan out in a half-circle. Joan Crawford had donned a robe with the same flair in one of her early gangster movies, *The Damned Don't Cry*, and Ruie Ann thought she favored the movie star.

She returned to the guest room and sat on the bed, crossing her arms over sagging breasts, impatiently waiting for the apology that never came. Instead, she felt the first of ten hacking blows to the top of her head and left temple. She screamed and struggled to fend off the attacker, grabbing hands, hair. Blood spurted and ran down her face and onto her neck and chest.

She fought hard and broke two fingers on her left hand and cut her right. She fell over onto the foot of the bed, soaking the mattress with blood. And then she felt hands around her ankles.

She was dragged off the mattress, face down across the hard floor, down the hallway, and across a rug that bunched under her. She raised her left arm, knocking books from a shelf in the den. Finally, she lay still, the metallic scent of the blood pooling under her head filling her nostrils. She felt something thrown over her, and seconds later, she heard the den door open and quietly close.

At first, the seventy-five-year-old widow didn't realize how badly she was injured, but she could feel the sticky blood on her neck and arms. Her head throbbed worse than any migraine she'd ever had, and when she tried to lift it, she couldn't. Her throat was dry, and she wished for a sip of water. Minutes passed before she lost consciousness, and her last thoughts were of how she would ever get rid of the blood stains in the showplace of Van Buren, Arkansas.

CHAPTER TWO

May 17, 1981

Sam Hugh Park awakened around eleven on Sunday morning with the sun shining behind old and uneven Venetian blinds. Hung over, as usual, he stumbled into the kitchen of the small house he rented from his mother. With a shaking hand, he reached for the bottle of vodka he kept in the refrigerator, took a long swallow, and immediately felt some relief.

He walked into the living room where his newest boy, Santos, was asleep on the couch. He tousled his long, black hair.

"Get up," he said and jabbed his ribs with his hand, but Santos only stirred slightly and rolled over. "Fuck it," Sam Hugh said.

He heated a cup of coffee in the microwave and walked out onto his small front porch. He realized he had slept in his clothes and noticed a semen stain on his yellow sweater. He briefly wondered whose it was.

Across the street at his mother's house, her morning paper still lay on the sidewalk where she demanded it be thrown.

"Mom hasn't gotten her paper yet?" he said aloud and then laughed, realizing he was talking to himself more and more these days. Ever since he'd lost his job as the youngest US prosecuting attorney of the Fifth District of the State of Arkansas, he found the most interesting conversations were those he had with himself.

He had made good money, but he spent it foolishly on liquor and entertainment with other homosexuals, sometimes supporting as many as three young men he had rescued from the county jails. Now he lived in one of his mother's three rent houses and hung his shingle out in the front bedroom. He did not have a thriving legal practice, but there weren't that many lawyers in Van Buren, so he billed enough clients that he was able to employ a secretary.

He went back inside and met Santos coming out of the bathroom.

"I tried to wake you up earlier," he said to the boy, who was clad only in his underwear.

Santos was currently Sam Hugh's favorite, and Santos wanted to keep it that way. He lived there rent-free, with all the beer and drugs he wanted.

"Got anything you want me to do today?" he asked.

"You can pick up the place. I had people in and out all night, but alas," he said with a chuckle, "I don't remember who they were."

"Anything else?"

Sam Hugh unzipped his pants. "Yeah."

A couple of hours later, after Santos had left to go horseback riding, Sam Hugh walked outside again and saw his mother's newspaper still lying where it had been earlier. He and his mother fought bitterly— and often—over his excessive drinking and fondness for young boys, but they always made up.

He had talked to her on the phone the night before and remembered the conversation.

"Oh, Sammie, I'm so tired from that bus trip to Cincinnati, but I think I got everything I need for my new book."

Sam Hugh knew she used trips for tax deductions, but he played along, mainly because he needed to borrow some money.

"Steamships on the Arkansas River should be interesting," he said, "but you need to take a break from it and relax."

"Oh, I have. I've been watching the *PTL* show, and Tammy Faye told the sweetest Memorial Day story. That's coming up, you know. Oh, yeah, there was a wonderful gospel trio from Kentucky on the show, too."

"I watched a movie on HBO. *Wholly Moses*. I laughed all the way through it. That short guy, Dudley Moore, was in it."

"You shouldn't watch movies that make fun of the Bible. I forbid it."

Oh, Jesus, he thought, as he remembered the phone conversation. *How long will I have to put up with her?*

Humming "Slow Hand" by the Pointer Sisters, he walked across the street with the keys to his mother's house in his hand and picked up the rolled newspaper, thick with ads from stores like Wild Bill Engle's Appliances that sold 19-inch television sets for $399.98 and under-the-counter dishwashers for $249.95. Hunt's Department Store advertised ankle strap sandals for $19.98 and a taffeta dress for $38.99.

He unlocked the kitchen door at the back of the house. There were two other entrances, but this was the one he used when he visited her.

"Mother?" he called. The house felt cold for such a warm afternoon. "Mother?"

He saw his mother's house shoes on the kitchen floor and thought that was strange. A sick feeling hit him that maybe she'd fallen down the basement stairs just off the kitchen, but he saw nothing suspicious there.

He stepped into the den and saw her body on the floor, partially covered with a yellow quilt or something like that, and for a second, a ridiculous thought popped into his head that she could be taking a nap. With her bare buttocks exposed, she lay on her stomach next to a wingback chair. Her bloody head was turned to the side, under which a good bit of blood pooled on the wooden floor.

He walked closer and knelt down for a better look. He felt lightheaded and thought he might faint. Or vomit. He felt bile rising into his throat, and he was desperate to get away from the sight on the floor. He hurried into his mother's kitchen and dialed the police.

"I've got an emergency here," he said. "Four eleven Fayetteville Road."

And then he went outside, sat down on the grass, and cried until the police arrived.

The body in the den

CHAPTER THREE

County Sheriff Trellon Ball received the call about the homicide of Ruie Ann Park shortly after he'd finished his Sunday dinner of a roast and potatoes and carrots. His wife, Ruby, had put the blue metal roaster in the oven before they left for Sunday school at the First Baptist Church. The Balls and their two daughters lived in Alma, a town even smaller than Van Buren, but both cities were in Crawford County.

Alma was also the home of a religious group that had moved to the area, founded by Susan Alamo and her husband, Tony. They'd built dormitory housing for their converts and a nice home for them to live in. Susan had grown up in a little community called Dyer, northeast of Alma, and had returned after becoming an evangelist with some followers out in California. Tony gathered up wayward souls to see the light and put them to work in a variety of businesses he started, such as home builders, restaurants, and even a clothing business that produced elaborate sequined costumes for performers to wear in Nashville and Hollywood.

Many people thought the Alamos were a cult and wanted nothing to do with them, but because they were all registered voters in

Crawford County, Trellon Ball courted them. He needed their votes for sheriff, and he got them. So did the mayor of Dyer, Fayette Peevy.

On Sheriff Ball's drive to Van Buren, he recalled the many times he'd seen Mrs. Park. Before she and her husband, Hugh, divorced, they'd published the local newspaper, *The Press Argus*. Hugh had died of a heart attack some years back. As far as he knew, Mrs. Park lived alone. He ran into her in the courthouse now and then when she was looking up abstracts or marriage licenses or divorce decrees or tax liens. She imagined herself the town historian and genealogist, and she was forever publishing articles in historical journals around the state.

What he remembered most was that she usually looked like she just woke up and forgot to comb her dyed, red hair. But she never forgot the bright-red lipstick or the rose rouge that circled her cheeks. Galoshes sometimes covered her feet, even on the sunniest of days.

The Park home was a lovely red brick with two white pillars on either side of the front porch. It sat near the top of Log Town Hill, as the locals called that section of Arkansas Highway 59, also named Fayetteville Street. The area was once called Signal Hill because signals were sent from the stagecoaches on the famous Butterfield Trail to the livery stable in town, estimating their arrival time. Wagons delivering the mail traveled this trail from Missouri to Memphis before being put out of business by the Pony Express, Indians, and marauding gangs of bushwhackers.

At the bottom of the hill sat the main street of sleepy little Van Buren, where the Frisco Train Station had been turned into a tourist attraction. Across the street was the Cottage Café, the gathering place for old men to have breakfast and hash over politics, and where, come Monday morning, they would all be talking about the murder of Ruie Ann Park.

Farther down Main and close to the Arkansas River, the Crawford County Courthouse sat, majestically surrounded by ancient oaks, complete with a fountain. It looked like pictures of genteel plantation homes in states deeper south than Arkansas.

But the Park home on top of Log Town Hill was not the picture of Southern gentility when Sheriff Ball turned in to the driveway. Several cars and trucks were already there, and yellow crime scene tape had been loosely strung around the back driveway. He parked behind the house in an area backed by thick woods. A brick sidewalk ran along the east side and joined a small porch supported by several rows of brick steps. He doubted anyone ever knocked on the front door, except for maybe a Mormon or a Jehovah's Witness.

Wayne Hicks, the assistant police chief of Van Buren, a tall, fat man with several chins, greeted the sheriff, who could stand to lose some weight himself.

Don Taylor, trim and muscled up, was an investigator with the Arkansas State Police. He wrote furiously in his notebook and didn't look up to acknowledge the sheriff. There was always a good bit of one-upmanship among the law enforcement agencies, and the sheriff quickly realized he was the last to arrive at the crime scene. He felt like a husband who is the last to know his wife is having an affair.

"Well, fill me in," the sheriff said in his most official voice.

"I got the call around one thirty p.m.," Hicks said. "The victim's son said he called his mother, and she hadn't answered, so he went across the street to check on her. He took his keys with him because he knew her doors would be locked. She was real careful about locking the doors, he said."

"And? Come on, man. What else?"

"He unlocked the kitchen door and found his mother dead in the den." Chief Hicks lowered his voice and pointed toward the man wearing black-rimmed glasses, leaning against the side of the house, smoking a cigarette. "You know who he is, don't you? That queer lawyer? Sam Hugh Park?"

"I know him, all right. I've been up to his house on some disturbance calls."

"I think he done it, don't you? Him or one of his queer friends."

Sheriff Ball shook his head hard from side to side. "Don't jump to conclusions, Hicks. Somebody might hear."

The sheriff nodded toward Garrick Feldman, the new owner of *The Press Argus,* who had written some unflattering columns about the sheriff department's connection with a local "religious cult."

"Sorry, Sheriff," Hicks said. "Nobody heard nothing I said. And you're right, you're absolutely right. I should watch what I say." Sweat ran down Hicks's cheeks and pooled along his shirt collar. Wet half-moons spread under his arms, and he kept reaching for his handkerchief to mop his brow. "This is really something," he said. "I'm so wired up, I feel like I might explode."

The sheriff hitched up his pants and tried to tuck in his white shirt. He still wore his Sunday shirt, and it was a little short and a little tight around his belly. He wished he had thought to change into his uniform. "Well," he said, "I guess I better look at the murder scene."

Sheriff Ball and six other officers, including Investigator Taylor, entered the house through the kitchen door. To the right was a refrigerator, a Harvest Gold model, with blood smeared on the door. Across from the refrigerator sat the stove, and on the floor in front of it, a pair of women's house shoes. A hallway led to the rest of the house.

Sheriff Ball let out an audible gasp. Mrs. Park lay on her stomach in the middle of the den, her left arm above her head. Her body was covered in blood, and under her head lay a large circle of what looked like red paint.

"It looks like somebody beat the hell out of her, especially on the top of her head. You agree?" the sheriff said to Taylor, but he got no response.

The sheriff asked another question. "Is that a Persian rug under her? With a *quilt* over her?"

Taylor still didn't comment.

The sheriff pulled on the waist of his pants again. Ruby told him she could always tell when he was nervous because he hitched up his pants.

"That looks like a pillow case and a napkin by her feet. How come?"

The sheriff realized Taylor was not listening to him, and he felt his face redden. He turned to Hicks and pointed to a long smear of blood.

"Let's see where that trail leads us."

They followed it to the east door, past a floral wingback chair and five or six encyclopedia books strewn on the hardwood floor. Treading carefully into a hallway, they entered the east bedroom, which looked to be a guest room because it was so neat and devoid of any pictures or knickknacks lying around. At the foot of the bed, which had no sheets or other covers, was another large circle of blood, and on the floor at the north side of the bed were other spots.

"Whoever killed her drug her into the den," the sheriff said, scratching his head. "But why? Why not leave her on the bed?"

He looked around the room that contained two dressers and a baby's cradle. A mirror hung over one dresser, and two bedside tables sat on either side of the bed. He supposed they were all expensive antiques, but what did he know about such things? He shopped at Sears if he wanted something really nice.

They walked through the rest of the house. The formal living room and dining room appeared to be used only for company. Pale-green satin drapes hung at the windows, where a spectacular view opened up on an often-photographed scene of the Arkansas River Bridge that connected Van Buren to Fort Smith.

The master bedroom was at the back of the house, across the patio from the kitchen. On a bookshelf built into the wall was an unopened black purse, and next to it, three or four framed pictures of young boys.

"Her purse wasn't taken, and her bed doesn't look like it's been slept in," the sheriff said. "The covers have been turned down, though. Like she was fixing to go to bed."

A blue telephone, a lamp with a fancy white shade, and some books sat on a table next to the bed. Hicks picked up the phone receiver, listened for the dial tone, and dropped it back in its cradle. He read aloud the titles of the books.

"*Lovely Lady* by Harold Robbins, *The Thorn Birds* by Colleen McCullough, and *Scruples* by Judith Krantz. Never heard of 'em," he said. "'Course, how would I know? I hate to read."

He thumbed through the books, looking for notes or scraps of paper, and placed them back where they were. "Boy, all these books around. Sure did read a lot."

The sheriff remembered his days in grade school, reading the Hardy Boys Mysteries, and when he got older, he had checked out all the Tarzan books at the little Alma Library.

"I guess she was a real bookworm."

They walked back to the den where Taylor stood with a camera in his hand, taking pictures. He had removed the bedspread, mattress pad, pillowcase, and a pillow from the body.

"Come on in, guys," he said to the sheriff. "I think that cover was on the bed. The murderer pulled it all off together when he pulled the body into the den. I think that Persian rug was on the den floor, and it just got jumbled in along with everything else."

The sheriff waited a minute before speaking, surprised but pleased that Taylor was including him.

"That sounds about right," he said with authority. "You think a man did it?"

"Looks like her left hand is broken, with some dark hairs clutched between her right thumb and forefinger," Taylor said.

"She tried to defend herself against a man. I'm pretty sure a woman couldn't have done it."

"Well," Hicks said. "She fought to the death trying to defend herself. Pretty good for an old woman."

CHAPTER FOUR

In Cabot, some two and a half hours east of Van Buren, Linda Martin, the adopted daughter of Ruie Ann Park, stood in her laundry room, folding clothes. On a table by the dryer, a bucket of whites soaked in water and Clorox.

An old portable radio sat on the windowsill, and Linda listened to the national news. The Cardinals and the Yankees and all the other major league baseball teams were threatening to strike. President Reagan and Nancy were at Camp David. A new, deadly disease was killing men, but doctors couldn't figure out why.

Her husband, Howard, peeked in on his way to the kitchen.

"Be sure to put Downy in with the rinse. I like the way it makes my socks feel."

"I always do, Howard." But she always didn't. That was one way she could get even with her bossy husband. He treated her just like her mother had. Like she didn't have a brain in her head and was lucky to have a place to live and food to eat.

She heard Howard in the kitchen, opening cabinet doors, closing them.

"Where's the Windex?" he yelled. "I want to clean the windows in the station wagon."

"Under the sink," she called. She wanted to scream, *Right where it always is, dumbass.* But she didn't.

Howard and their oldest son, Carl, had gone to a Boy Scout camp the night before. The middle son, Harry, had spent the night with his granny in Cabot, and the youngest, an eighteen month old, was left with his mom. And now, all three were sound asleep in the den in front of the TV.

Linda should be happy. She did, indeed, have a bed to sleep in, food to eat, and clothes to wear—the mantra her husband had borrowed from her mother and now preached to her. The only difference was that Howard had thrown in three sons to add to the things she should be thankful for.

Linda was standing, looking out the window, when her husband touched her shoulder.

"Hey," he said. "What you thinking about so hard? That's unusual for you."

"Oh, I was thinking how much I love to do laundry."

Howard actually chuckled. "When's supper?"

She turned off the radio and took the folded clothes into the master bedroom. She placed Howard's underwear in one drawer, his socks and handkerchiefs in another. On her side of the closet, she hung up the navy blue skirt she had worn to church that morning.

Howard selected all her clothes, just as her mother had. But the clothes her mother had selected were what she liked, not what was popular with teenagers. Sometimes her mother had picked out patterns and material at Fort Smith's Boston Store basement for Mrs. Riley to make clothes for her. The same seamstress who fashioned underwear out of the red rayon Ruie Ann purchased for herself.

Linda laughed out loud, thinking about her mother's red underwear. Nothing could make that woman sexy.

Linda placed her clean cotton panties and bras in a small dresser drawer, checking to make sure the love letter from a divorce client of Howard's was still safely hidden. She had found the letter in a jacket pocket of his blue suit, the one he wore to court. *Missing you on Monday,* the letter read. *Longing for you on Tuesday. Happy on Wednesday.* Linda had felt sick when she'd read the letter. She knew who Judy was. She was the kind of woman men liked. Blonde. Giggled at everything, funny or not. Always wore tight jeans and teased her hair like Dolly Parton. She'd been married before.

Linda had begun to suspect something was going on between the two when Judy, the client, started to call Howard at home so often. Normally, Howard wouldn't accept calls at home. "Please call the office tomorrow" was his standard response to a call after hours.

Linda sat on the bench at the foot of the bed and looked out at her world of Winnwood Heights. She spent hours watering the newly sodded yard, and her home was something she took pride in. She heard the familiar Sunday afternoon sounds of lawnmowers and weed eaters. Across the street, the Jackson's daughter, a champion high school tennis player, bounced a tennis ball on the driveway. Her daddy had bought her a new wooden Chris Evert racquet for her birthday. These were all good, happy people, and she longed to be one of them.

The phone on the bedside table rang, and Linda grabbed it after the first ring.

"Hello," she said.

Her brother identified himself and began weeping.

Linda sat down on the bed. "Sam Hugh, what's wrong?"

"It's Mother. She's dead."

"Dead? What happened? When? Oh, Sam Hugh, Sam Hugh, Sam Hugh."

"Someone killed her, Linda. I found her in the den with blood everywhere, all over her head. Horrible thing to see, Linda. Horrible, horrible, horrible."

"Who killed her?" Linda could tell her brother was drunk, but he'd never be so drunk he'd make up something like this. "Where are you?"

"I'm home now, but the police are still at Mother's. They think I did it. I can tell by the way they look at me."

"When did it happen?"

"Last night or early this morning."

"Oh, my God!"

"The state police are here. The sheriff and that idiot Wayne Hicks. All the people from the newspaper. Even the goddamn TV cameras are here now."

"We'll be there just as soon as we can."

Linda hung up the phone. She put her hand over her mouth and wailed in a low voice that grew louder and louder.

From outside, Howard heard her and rushed into the bedroom. He sat on the bed beside Linda.

"What the hell happened?"

"Sam Hugh just called. Mother's dead. He found her. Someone killed her."

"What? Who would kill her? What did Sam Hugh say again? Tell me without crying."

"My mother's been killed," she wailed.

"Shh, shh, don't frighten the children."

"I can't believe it. All these years I've hated her, but now she's dead. I don't know what to think."

"You need to lie down."

"I don't want to lie down, Howard. Will you get me a Coke? I feel like I'm going to be sick."

"Okay. Stay right here. I'll get a wet washcloth."

Linda sobbed again, but now in deep gulps, sometimes losing her breath.

"It's not true," she said over and over. "How can it be true?"

Howard came back with her Coke, took a sip himself, and then handed it to her. He rubbed her face with a wet cloth, almost causing her to spill the bottle. She hated this act of love and sympathy. Linda wanted to tell him to stop it, that she knew it was just an act. She wanted to scream and tell him she had found the love letter and knew about Judy.

Instead, she found the courage to smile and play the game.

"You're so good to me. It's all so unbelievable," she said, resting the Coke bottle against her cheek. "I used to wish she would die. Then, when Daddy died, I thought God was punishing me for those thoughts." She looked at Howard and then asked, "Who could have done it?"

"Let's don't think about that now."

Linda had met her husband at the University of Arkansas in Fayetteville in the early 1960s. He'd been her first and only boyfriend. She had often chuckled, remembering how dumb he looked with his short Navy haircut compared to the other college boys. She and Howard had belonged to a group who went to church parties instead of fraternity or sorority parties.

Linda returned to the horrible present when Carl and Harry ran into the room, wondering why their mom was crying.

With their sandy hair, they resembled their father, but their slender facial features were more like hers.

"Mom, what's wrong?" Harry asked. "Are you sick?"

Howard put an arm around each son. "Mom is sad. We've just found out Parky died. That's why Mom is crying. We have to go to Van Buren to see about things and visit with your Uncle Sam Hugh."

Harry's bottom lip quivered, and his eyes filled with tears. He barely knew his grandmother, but he understood it was a bad thing to die.

Howard patted Harry on the back. "I'll see if Mrs. Coleman can come and stay with you boys." He looked at his watch, picked up the

19

phone, and dialed the number he had memorized. "She should be home from church now."

Howard always took control of everything. *He* decided if they needed a babysitter. *He* decided if there was a civic event they should attend together. Linda wasn't allowed to get a sitter during the day, even to get her hair done.

She slowly stood and picked up the baby, who had slept through her loud weeping and toddled in looking for her. She hugged him tightly. The reality of her life, as unhappy as it was, was that her sons needed her, and she vowed to always take care of them. Bobby was only eighteen months old, and he loved his mama—much more than his daddy, Linda knew for certain. Howard wasn't a cuddly sort of father.

She put the baby on her hip. "Yes, you call Mrs. Coleman. That's a good idea. And I'll get us packed. I imagine we'll need to stay several days."

Howard put his hands on his waist and stretched backward. Lately, he'd been bothered by his back. He guessed it was the result of sitting at his desk and working hard for his growing family.

"I've got to check on something at the office. I'll take the little red car."

"Take the station wagon," Linda said.

"What does it matter? You didn't drive the Chevette while I was gone, did you?"

"Please, please, Howard," Linda said, her voice rising. "Must you quiz me? My God, I've just found out my mother's been murdered. I know you don't want me to drive your little red car."

Howard looked at Linda, frowning, his nostrils flaring, like they always did when he was angry.

"Wait just a minute here. You're upset, I know." He stared directly into her eyes. "But that's no reason to scream at me. I'm tired. I slept in a tent all night long on the hard ground. Now, I've got to drive to Van Buren, talk to the police, and see your brother, who will no doubt be drunk."

"Don't say things about Sam Hugh. He's all I've got left now. Besides the boys."

"What about me? Don't I count around here?"

"Of course you count," Linda said, almost in a whisper. "You've always counted most of all."

He patted Linda's shoulder. "Okay, then, let's simmer down."

Linda hated for him to pat her shoulder. It was like he was patting a dog.

She watched Howard drive out the driveway in the 1980 Chevette that was owned by the law firm, ostensibly used only by Howard in connection with his law practice. Tax reasons, he said. Linda suspected he drove to the office to call his girlfriend.

She telephoned her neighbor, Martha Gray.

"Something horrible has happened. My mother's been killed." She listened as her friend made the appropriate responses to the news of the murder. "Will you please tell everyone for me? Tell the new minister I'll have to cancel the cookout Wednesday night."

She made a list of things to do before she left, and then she made a list of what to pack. She would wear the navy suit she wore for Easter to the funeral. Jeans and short-sleeved shirts would do for the rest of the time.

Howard's half of the closet was full of clothes—suits together, sport jackets together, dress pants together, short-sleeve shirts together, long-sleeve shirts together, jeans together. Even the ties hung separated by colors on the wooden tie rack.

She knew she could never choose the right tie with the right suit. Let him pack his own damn clothes.

Linda heard the doorbell and ran to answer it. She held out her arms to Mrs. Coleman.

"Thank you so much for coming. I don't know what I'd do without you."

"Oh, Linda. I'm so sorry about your mother. Such an awful thing." She pulled a white lace handkerchief from under the sleeve of her church dress and handed it to Linda. "Have you heard anything else?"

"No, nothing. We'll know more when we get there. My brother lives there."

Mrs. Coleman was a member of the Cabot Church of Christ. She wanted to ask what church Linda's mother had attended. Instead, she asked, "Was your mother right with the Lord?"

Linda laughed. "If Mother were here, she'd ask if the Lord was right with her."

Mrs. Coleman didn't know what to say to that, so she asked a simpler question.

"What can I do to help you?"

"You can fold the clothes in the dryer. The boys can show you where things go. And I have a couple of things soaking in some bleach water. Rinse those out and put them in with the basket ready to go in the washer."

When Howard returned from his office, he greeted Mrs. Coleman with a friendly hug.

"I'll be home right after the funeral, which should be in a few days. Linda will probably stay longer, so if you can plan on staying at least a week, I'd appreciate it."

"I can stay as long as you like. I've got my suitcase in the car." She smiled and said, "Are the children upset? Did they know their grandmother well?"

"They only saw her a few times a year. I'm afraid Mrs. Park wasn't the grandmotherly type. The children got on her nerves."

Linda called to Howard from the bedroom.

"Come get your clothes together. We need to hurry. I don't want Sam Hugh to have to face all those people alone."

As Howard reached for a navy suit and red tie out of the closet, he said, "Don't worry about Sam Hugh. I'm sure he's well anesthetized by now."

Linda shot Howard an angry look. "Yes, that's what I'm afraid of."

"And I'm going to lose at least three days of work, and with gas at close to a dollar and a half, and add in what I'll have to pay Mrs. Coleman. Damn it, this is going to cost a hell of a lot of money."

"I'm sorry someone murdered my mother, and I'm sorry it's going to cost you money."

He gave her a hateful look, and they didn't talk to each other on the entire trip to Van Buren. Linda was glad because she needed time to think. Time to figure out some things.

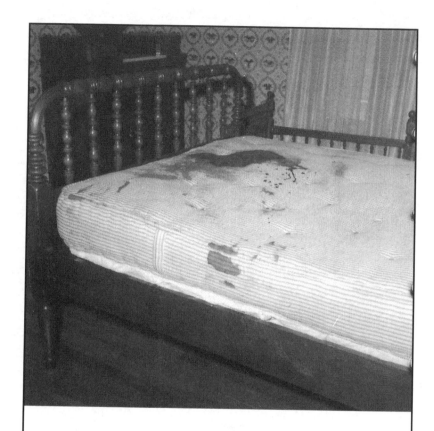

**Bloodstained mattress
in the guest bedroom**

CHAPTER FIVE

Rusty and Linda Myers were headed home from the First Presbyterian Church when they saw the commotion at Ruie Park's home. They pulled in and parked behind a truck Rusty recognized as belonging to the publisher of *The Press Argus*. He told his wife to stay in the car with their children.

"What's going on?" he asked when he saw Feldman.

"A murder. Ruie Ann Park is inside with her head bashed in."

"What? I can't believe it!"

"The cops are inside now. They're all so excited they're about to piss their pants."

Rusty felt like he'd been kicked in the stomach. He'd known Ruie all his life. Sam Hugh had been the best man at his wedding. They'd been fraternity brothers at the U of A.

"Where's Sam Hugh?"

Feldman nodded toward the patio at the back of the house. "He's over there. He's in bad shape. He found her body. Poor guy. I can't imagine what that was like for him. She was on her stomach with her bare butt showing."

Rusty took off his glasses, and then he put them back on.

"Had she been raped?"

"They don't think so. She was in her gown and robe and had pin curls in her hair."

"Have you been inside?"

"Oh, no. I got my information from Chief Hicks. You know him. He can't keep his mouth shut."

Rusty shook Feldman's hand, thanked him for the information, and walked toward his best friend.

Sam Hugh had on the clothes he'd worn the night before to supper—a yellow sweater and dark-brown slacks. He was tall and thin and looked good in his clothes. He used to be a dapper dresser, but he didn't look dapper today.

"Hi, buddy," Sam Hugh said, grabbing Rusty's hand. He was a good bit taller than Rusty and just a few years older, but he looked like a weakened old man. "I found her. Did you know that? God, she looked so old and so bloody. Her arms were all askew, and bless her heart, she wasn't wearing panties. She'd be humiliated to know how she ended up."

"Got any ideas, Sam Hugh? I mean, who could have done this?"

Sam Hugh raised both arms, his hands flat.

"I don't know, man. But I tell you, I'm scared. Scared shitless. That's a mean son of a bitch who'd kill an old lady like my mom."

"Can I do something for you, Sam Hugh? Call someone? Does your sister know?"

He took off his glasses and wiped his eyes on the sleeve of his sweater.

"She's on her way."

"Well, when she gets here, y'all are welcome to stay with us. Tonight, tomorrow, any time you need to get away from . . . all this," he said, waving his arm. "We'll fix some sandwiches or something." He turned and looked toward his car. "I better go tell her what happened and get the kids home. We've been to church and got Kentucky Fried Chicken in the car."

"Yeah, sure. Can you believe this shit, Rusty? Can you believe it?"

Rusty walked back to his car, and when he saw his wife in the front seat and his three children in the back, safe and sound and free from anything ugly in this world, he began to cry. He climbed into the car and rested his forehead on the steering wheel. After reaching for his wife's hand and squeezing it with a secret message that said "I'll tell you what happened when we get home," he backed around a police car and pulled out onto Fayetteville Street.

Linda Myers turned to the backseat.

"I'm ready for lunch, are you guys?" A chorus of yeses rang out loudly from three sets of lungs. "All right, Daddy. Let's feed these kids some chicken and mashed potatoes and gravy."

When they returned to their home, the phone was ringing. The news of Ruie Ann Park's murder had spread quickly. High school classmates called. Methodist church members, who had sung hymns while Sam Hugh played the organ, called. Merchants who had benefitted from Sam Hugh's membership in the Van Buren Urban Renewal Commission called and wanted to know where to send flowers, where to send memorials, where to send food. Members of the King Opera House players called and wanted to see what they could do for their founder. By the middle of the afternoon, Rusty took the phone off the hook and went outside with his wife to watch the kids play on their new swing set.

After Rusty and Linda read to their children and listened to their prayers that Sunday night, he checked the windows and doors for the second time before they turned out the light and crawled into their bed. Exhausted from the phone calls, the couple held hands under the covers and discussed how they might best help Sam Hugh and his sister.

"I don't want Sam Hugh and Linda seeing their mother's blood every time they go inside the house," Rusty said.

"Yes, I've already thought about that. I'll clean the house. I want to do that for Sam Hugh. He's been a good friend to us."

Rusty squeezed his wife's hand hard and thought he'd never loved her more than he did at that very moment.

CHAPTER SIX

Sam Hugh hung up the phone after telephoning his sister a second time. Howard had grabbed the phone from her.

"This is Howard, and you do not need to call us again. We will be there as soon as we can. And don't be drunk when we get there."

"The prick," Sam Hugh said, pitching the address book on the floor. He'd known Howard when they were in law school together at the U of A, but they were never friends. Sam Hugh was brilliant, and it took two tries for Howard to pass the bar exam.

"Who's a prick?" Santos asked. He'd returned from horseback riding, seen all the cars around Ruie Ann's house, and rushed to Sam Hugh's house. He finished off a beer and lit a joint.

"Put that goddamn weed out, you goddamn fool. Don't you know the police are across the street? They'll be coming over here to ask me some more questions."

"I thought you'd already talked to them."

"The police think I did it, Santos."

"Oh, no," Santos said, sounding like he finally understood the gravity of the situation.

"Oh, yes, indeed."

Santos took the rest of his stash and placed it in a leather coin purse. He dropped it inside a Kleenex box that sat on top of the television set and proceeded to fan away the smoke with his hands.

"That's not going to do any good," Sam Hugh said. "Turn on the ceiling fan and bring me a drink."

When Santos returned from the kitchen and sat the drink of straight vodka over ice by his side, Sam Hugh was on the phone. He was crying.

"Who you talking to, Sam Hugh?" whispered Santos.

He put the phone to his chest. "It's one of Mom's friends from the Methodist Church." He let out another long sob and spoke again into the phone. "I loved my mother. You know I did. I can't believe anyone would want to kill her. She didn't keep cash, and the two renters pay on the first of the month."

Santos continued to listen as Sam Hugh declared his love for his mother. Sam Hugh loved her, Santos knew, but they fought like cats and dogs, mostly over the boys Sam Hugh took in. She said they ruined the neighborhood. But for some reason, Ruie Ann (she had insisted Santos call her Ruie Ann) seemed to like him, and she had even invited him to Thanksgiving dinner last November. In fact, it seemed that sometimes Ruie Ann approved of her son helping the wayward souls, as she called them.

Just as Sam Hugh predicted, Don Taylor of the Arkansas State Police knocked on the front door. Santos let him in before he left to sit outside on the front steps. Through the screen door, he could hear the men talking.

"When did you last see your mother alive?"

"It must have been around four thirty on Saturday afternoon. She stopped by after her walk with Marie Thompson."

"Who's Marie Thompson?"

"Her friend who lives in the neighborhood."

"Okay. You happen to know her address?"

"I think it's 313 or maybe 315 Fayetteville Street."

"Okay, we'll talk to her."

"I told my mother I saw Rusty and Linda Myers at the grocery store, and they had invited me for supper. I was getting ready to leave when she came by."

"And how long did you stay at your friends' house?"

"I got home around seven o'clock. Early, because I wanted to watch *Wholly Moses* on cable. I called my mother, and she said she was going to watch *PTL*."

"That religious station?"

"Yeah, she watches it all the time. *Watched* it all the time, I guess I should say."

"Was that the last time you talked to her?"

"No, I called her after the movie, and she told me she was getting ready for bed. We said good-night, and that was around ten or ten thirty."

"Were you alone when you watched the movie?"

"Some friends dropped by, but they didn't like the movie, so they left."

"I'll need to get their names from you. But that can wait. And you heard nothing suspicious last night? Did you see a strange car?"

"No, just like I already told the sheriff. I saw absolutely nothing out of the ordinary last night. Mother keeps her house locked at all times."

"Who has keys?"

"Me, her, and my sister, Linda."

"Where does Linda live?"

"Cabot, not far from Little Rock. She and her husband are on the way up here now."

"I know where Cabot is, Sam Hugh."

Santos watched as Ruie Ann Park's body was loaded into a black Suburban. Sam Hugh had told him earlier they were sending her

31

body to Little Rock. He was glad Sam Hugh was inside and hadn't seen what he'd just seen. It made him sick with fear to think there was someone around who would kill a little lady like Ruie Ann. From outside, he heard a chair scrape across the hardwood floor, and Taylor soon opened the door onto the porch.

Santos stood up.

"Your name? You live here?"

"Off and on," Santos replied after he'd told the officer his name. "I do landscaping for Sam Hugh and anything else he needs done." He didn't like this man. He especially didn't like the sneer on his face.

"Santos, were you here last night?"

"For a little while, around five thirty or so, but I left to pick up Jackie. I brought her back here, and we watched a movie with Sam Hugh, but we didn't like it, so we left. But we came back because I realized I didn't have any money, so I asked Sam Hugh for five dollars, but he gave me ten. Then me and Jackie left and went to her house. I came home about five on Sunday morning and crashed on the divan. I got up around noon, I guess."

Detective Taylor turned the page on his notebook and asked, "Anyone else at Sam Hugh's?"

"Gary was in and out on Saturday."

"Who's Gary, and who's this Jackie? Do they live here with Sam Hugh, too?"

"Gary Shoop does sometimes. Not Jackie."

"This Jackie's a guy or girl?"

"Girl."

"Why's she hanging around with a bunch of queers?"

Santos looked across the street at all the cops milling around. He could feel the sweat making a circle under his arms.

"We're all just friends," Santos said.

Taylor laughed and closed his notebook and stuck it in his front pocket.

"Sure you are. And Mr. Sam Hugh Park doles out the money for sexual favors. Am I correct? No need to answer."

Santos watched Taylor trot down the steps like he had some place real important to be. He turned around and pointed a finger at Santos.

"Don't go anywhere. We'll want to talk some more with you. And your *friends*, as well. But the next time we talk, it will be at the sheriff's office."

Taylor walked across the street, climbed over the yellow tape that blocked the driveway, and disappeared into what Sam Hugh had always called the "Winter Palace." He'd asked him why he called it that, but Santos didn't really understand the reason.

"Read the book, *Shadow over the Winter Palace*," Sam Hugh explained. "It's about the Russian Czar Nicholas II and his crazy wife." Of course, Santos never read the book, not being a history buff like Sam Hugh was.

Santos walked back into the house where Sam Hugh sat in a brown corduroy recliner that his mother said should be given to the rescue mission under the bridge.

"They think I did it, Santos."

Sam Hugh was clearly on his way to being falling down drunk, and Santos felt sorry for him.

"The goddamned cops think I killed my own mother."

"Nah, Sam Hugh. That Taylor fucker thinks I did it. Or Gary maybe."

Sam Hugh began wailing, wailing like Santos had seen Comanche women do in cowboy movies when their husbands were killed. He pounded his fist against the chair arm.

"They would like nothing else than to get me off this hill, but I won't give them the chance. I'll leave. They can't arrest me. I didn't kill my mother!"

Sam Hugh Park continued to drink, but now from the gallon bottle of Ancient Age delivered earlier by his personal delivery man,

Bill Spradley. Spradley lived off Highway 64, between Van Buren and Alma, and owned a liquor store in Fort Smith on Midland Boulevard. Crawford County was dry, all right, and liquor stores were closed on Sunday in Fort Smith, but if you knew who to call, nearly everything you desired, legal or not, could be delivered to your front door.

CHAPTER SEVEN

Howard drove slowly up the drive of 410 Fayetteville Road and parked in the driveway to the Park home. He looked at his watch and saw that the trip had taken not quite three hours. Linda looked straight ahead, avoiding the stares of the people clustered around the edges of the roped-off yard. She took a damp handkerchief out of her pocket and turned it over and over in her hand. She dreaded seeing the neighbors, the police, the newspaper reporters, and most of all, her brother.

The sheriff watched from the backyard, then rushed out to the driveway and opened the car door for Linda. He held out his large hand and gently helped her out of the car.

Linda took the sheriff's hand and accepted the whispered "sorry 'bout your mom" greeting. She saw Sam Hugh leaning against a police car. His face was drawn and pale.

"Oh, Sam Hugh, it's so unbelievable."

"I know. I keep going home and then coming back here. It doesn't seem true." He put his arm around her and said, "You look worn out." He hadn't seen her since Thanksgiving, and her frailty shocked him.

Something was bothering her, and it wasn't just being the mother of three little boys.

"Hello, Sam Hugh," Howard said as he walked over. Sam Hugh slowly unwrapped one arm from his sister's waist and offered his hand. Neither man said anything. Only a handshake and a polite nod.

Sheriff Ball noticed this lack of friendship between Sam Hugh and his brother-in-law from Cabot. He took a notebook from his shirt pocket and made a notation of this coolness.

"Sheriff, if it's okay with you," Sam Hugh said, "I'll take Linda and Howard up to my house. I know you want to talk to Linda, but let her catch her breath before you start your interrogation."

"I do need to talk to you, ma'am," said the sheriff, "and I know you want me to find your mom's killer just as soon as I can. You go on up to your brother's, and I'll be there directly."

They crossed the street and walked up on Sam Hugh's porch. His front door stood ajar. Time had warped it, and half-hearted efforts to repair it had not been successful.

It was one of many things Sam Hugh had let go.

"Welcome to my humble abode," he said as he pushed the door open for Linda.

"I see you still haven't repaired the front door," Howard said.

"Nope, why should I? Who would want anything I have?"

"I would suggest that, in light of what happened at your mother's house, yours should be locked, for God's sake."

Sam Hugh turned on the window air conditioner in the small living room.

"Sorry it's so hot in here. It'll cool off soon. I usually just keep the one in the kitchen on and stay in the back."

The house smelled of stale beer and cigarettes. Howard and Linda watched as Sam Hugh picked up a pillow and an old quilt from the couch and threw them in the corner. The dusty floor showed bare footprints, and dust balls lined the baseboard.

Howard ran a finger across the coffee table.

"Why don't you hire someone to come in and clean this place?"

The air conditioner hummed while the three sat silently in the hot room. Howard unbuttoned the top two buttons of his shirt and fanned himself like an old woman might do. Sam Hugh and Linda looked at each other, and he winked.

Sam Hugh moved from his chair over to the couch next to Linda. They had never been close growing up. Once he had pulled the head off her favorite doll, and later, when she'd reached her awkward teenage years, he had called her names like Olive Oyl and Fig Newton. Sam Hugh was allowed to drive the family car, but she wasn't. She had to study hard to maintain the A's and B's that her mother demanded. He never studied and always made A's, and all his teachers thought he was a genius. Ruie Ann Park thought there was no one in the world as smart as her Sammie. And through the years at home in Van Buren, Linda knew she was the inferior child, and she buried her resentment and anger deep inside while her brother ignored her and her mother controlled her every move.

Linda could smell the whiskey on his breath and the familiar sour smell that told her he had drunk too much the night before, and she wondered what damage their mother had inflicted upon both of them.

"Did you hear anything last night?" Linda asked.

"No, I had some friends drop by. I was watching a movie, but nobody but me liked it."

"You'll need witnesses. I guess you know that," Howard said.

"Huh?" Sam Hugh rose from the couch and placed his hands on his hips. "You think I'm a suspect, do you?"

"Of course I do, and you know it, too. The whole town knows about your arguments with Ruie Ann. They were plenty loud. Hell, the neighbors called the police twice."

"Who told you that lie?"

"Your mother called and told us all about you and your queer friends. She told us about the drinking and the pot, too."

"You've always been a real pain in the ass, Howard. I suggest you shut your mouth."

Linda pulled on her brother's hand. "Come on, you two. Please don't fight. Not now, for God's sake."

CHAPTER EIGHT

Sheriff Ball sat in the front seat of his Ford. He started the engine and turned on the air conditioner. It was hot. Real hot for mid-May.

He watched the sun set and wished Ruby could be here to see this spectacular scene. The Arkansas River sparkled in the sunlight as it ribboned its way between Van Buren and Fort Smith. The three bridges—one for trains to use, the others for cars—spanned the river majestically from this viewpoint. He'd once met the man, a Mr. Barber, who had designed and built the middle bridge, the one the locals used most. At Christmas time, in the sand along the river bank, Arkhola Sand and Gravel Company put up the Three Wise Men. In blue lights. It was impressive. Everyone said so. He and Ruby always took the girls to see the sight.

He was nervous about interrogating two lawyers, but he looked forward to it anyway. He'd taken classes given by the state police and gone to a convention or two in Dallas. Still, he needed time to think and formulate his questions.

Sam Hugh had started off his legal career with a bang. Senator William Fulbright—everyone said he owed a favor to his father, Hugh Park—had gotten him a job as an assistant United States prosecuting attorney, with offices in the federal court house in Fort Smith. He hadn't stayed there long, maybe a year or so, and then he'd opened up an office in his home. Everyone knew he was smart, some said brilliant. The smartest man in Crawford County. He'd heard that Sam Hugh Park had invested in real estate around the county, and his law practice wasn't that busy. Maybe he needed money.

Maybe he should wait till tomorrow to question him, when he was hung over. Yes, he decided, he'd tell Sam Hugh to be at his office at eight on Monday morning. But then, thinking how early eight would come, he changed it to nine o'clock. He took out the notebook he always carried in his shirt pocket and began to write. He wrote "Sam Hugh Park" on the top of one page and numbered down one through ten.

Then he turned the page and did the same for Linda and Howard. They were husband and wife, but he had a hunch they weren't happily married.

Linda seemed to rely on Sam Hugh for support, instead of her husband. The sheriff felt sorry for her. She was such a cute little thing. When you looked at her face, all you saw were those big brown eyes, frightened eyes that seemed to be on the lookout for something about to happen. She was like the kittens that lived in his tool shed. They accepted his food but were cautious of any petting or touching.

The car radio sputtered, and a familiar voice called his name. He listened to his dispatcher and then answered, "Tell Ruby I don't know when I'll get home for supper."

He hated to miss a meal with his family. Leftover roast beef sandwiches would soon be on the table, but he couldn't make it, not with the most important investigation of his career waiting for him.

He rolled down the window, switched off the ignition, and got out of the car. He hitched up his pants and walked toward the house occupied by the dead woman's son.

"Most logical suspect I can see," he said out loud as he stepped over a large pecan branch that lay on the side of the road.

Sam Hugh answered the knock and invited the sheriff inside. He didn't ask the tall man to sit down. This wasn't a friendly chat but an investigation, and he would treat it as such.

"Now then, if you folks will bear with me, I'll get this out of the way and let you get on to taking care of things. First of all, let me say that your mother's body has been taken to Little Rock for an autopsy. Now, since it's Sunday, they won't do it till tomorrow. I don't know how many they'll have to do, since it's a weekend and all. Little Rock does all the autopsies for the state, and if there was a lot of wrecks and drownings, then things could get piled up. We'll just have to hope for the best."

"Will you notify us as soon as you hear something?" Linda asked.

"Of course. Will y'all stay here with your brother?"

Linda looked at Howard and waited for him speak.

"We'd better stay at a motel," she finally said. "I'll go call . . . what's the name of that one on the highway?"

"Just let me know one way or the other," said the sheriff. "Now, tell me, before I leave, where each of you were last night from dark until morning. Sam Hugh, I'll start with you."

"I was here all night. I had some friends over, but I didn't hear any screams or loud noises from my mother's house. I have no idea who might have wanted her dead. I don't know if she had any enemies. And that, Sheriff Ball, is all I intend to say on the subject." Sam Hugh then turned his back to the sheriff, winked at the astonished Howard, and went into the kitchen.

Howard cleared his throat. "Sheriff, I must apologize for my brother-in-law. I assure you that my wife and I will be more cooperative."

"That's all right, Mr. Martin. If Mr. Park doesn't want to be helpful, that's his own business."

"You don't think Sam Hugh killed our mother?" Linda asked. "He wouldn't do that. He was her own flesh and blood. They had a very special relationship, one that went way beyond the normal mother-son."

"What do you mean by that exactly?"

Linda pursed her lips, pausing to look for the correct words to explain their relationship.

"Well, he was very, very special in her eyes. She thought he was perfect in every way. She never stayed mad at him more than an hour, no matter what he had done or said."

"Where were *you* last night?" asked the sheriff.

"Why, I was home, of course. My husband and our oldest went camping."

"Where did you go camping, Mr. Martin?"

"We went on a Boy Scout camping trip to a nearby lake."

"Linda, do you have any witnesses to verify your alibi?"

Linda looked at Howard and began to cry once more.

"Sheriff, my wife is understandably upset. Our neighbors can tell you Linda was home last night. I'm sure there were lights on all over the house. She gets a little spooked when I'm gone and turns on all the lights."

"And how do you know that for sure?"

"Sheriff, that's exactly what I did," Linda said. "The baby and I sat outside before it got dark, took our baths, and went to bed."

"When did you last see your mother, Linda?" the sheriff asked in a gentle tone of voice. He sensed that Linda was what his wife would call a "basket case."

"We were here on Thanksgiving."

"I'm trying to get things straight in my mind, Linda. Can you help me out, if you will? Your mother and father were divorced? And before that, they owned *The Press Argus*?"

"Yes, sir. My father died in 1974, but he'd remarried. His wife still lives here, I believe." Linda looked through the kitchen doorway at Sam Hugh and then back again at the sheriff. "We're not close, and I've never known much about her."

"And you were adopted?"

"Yes, but not until I was twenty."

"Sheriff," interrupted Howard, "my wife was probably closer to her father. The divorce was very traumatic for everyone, but especially for Linda because she was devoted to her father. Her mother insisted on Linda's loyalty. Sam Hugh's, too, of course. She drew a line in the sand and forbade her children to step over it."

Forbade? *Forbade*? Was Howard trying to impress him with fancy words?

"I see. Divorce is always bad, but sometimes it's the only solution."

"What else do you need to know, Sheriff?" Howard asked, as he protectively placed his arm around his wife.

"Did your mother have any men friends?"

"No, never. At least none that I ever knew about. I really believe she liked living alone and having things her own way. She would have liked for Sam Hugh to live with her, but he wanted to have his own place," she said.

"I need a list of your mother's friends. Sometimes friends know more about a person than their family does."

"Sam Hugh would know better than me," Linda said.

Turning toward the kitchen and catching Sam Hugh's eye, she said, "Come in here, please. The sheriff needs to know the names of Mother's friends."

Sheriff Ball jotted down the things Linda had told him. Sam Hugh stood nervously, leaning to one side and then to the other, waiting.

The sheriff turned back several pages and read what he'd written. His lips moved as he read, an action both Linda and Sam Hugh noticed.

He looked at Sam Hugh, then his sister, and back to Sam Hugh.

"If you're ready to be helpful, I would like to know the names of your mother's friends."

"My mother was active in the local historical society. Those ladies would be considered acquaintances but not good friends," Sam Hugh said with a loud sigh.

Linda chewed on a fingernail. "I don't think Mother had any good friends. Oh, yes, there was a book club, too."

"Was your mother the kind of lady who was careful about locking the doors at night? Would she have opened the door to a stranger?"

"Mother was extremely careful," Linda replied after glancing at her brother.

The sheriff scratched his head, another nervous habit he'd picked up in his youth, and took out his pen and began to write.

"Now, Linda, I want you and your brother to walk down with me to your mom's house. I want y'all to look around and see if you can tell if anything is missing."

"Do I have to go?"

"Well, if you want us to find out who killed your mother. We don't know if it was a robbery or what."

Linda sighed and reached for her brother's hand. "Okay, I'll go."

The sheriff walked ahead and gave instructions to his deputy. The smell of exhaust fumes from idling motors hung heavily in the air. Cars were everywhere, full of curiosity-seekers wanting to see where a real murder was committed.

A white wrought-iron bench sat between two empty flower pots.

"Why do you suppose Mother bought this bench?" Sam Hugh asked. "Have you ever seen anyone sit on it?"

"Oh, she thought it was 'Old South.' She bought it after her first trip to Natchez and Vicksburg."

Sam Hugh nodded. He well remembered all the trips they'd taken. One in particular was most unpleasant. The family had traveled in a truck. "Roughing it" his mother had called it. He and Linda wore identical shirts made out of puffy nylon that could be easily washed. They rode in the back of the truck, facing the cars behind them.

"Remember the time I wanted to play jacks here? We had a big row over it," Linda said. "She said I was too old, and I'd scratch the concrete. I remember how good the cool concrete felt on my legs."

"I should have helped you out with her," whispered Sam Hugh, shaking his head and looking down at his feet. "She wouldn't let you do anything. I remember how you cried over the ribbons for the Rainbow Girl's Dance."

"I guess that's when I gave up. She said I didn't know how to choose colors. God, all the other girls had strapless formals with tons and tons of net. Miss Stratton made mine, and Mother picked out the pattern."

"I hated the piano recitals the most," Sam Hugh said. "One boy and a dozen girls."

"What happened to us? What happened that we should end up here, just the two of us, with Dad and now Mother gone?"

Linda raised her head to catch the unexpected cool breeze. She licked her forefinger and held it up.

"Feels like rain," she said with a nervous laugh. "Remember how Dad used to do that?"

"Mother ruined him. He couldn't please her. That's why he stayed away all the time. She never gave him a moment's peace. A real ball-buster."

"I can't remember his new wife's name."

"Me, either. I hope she made him happy."

"Can a person make another person happy? I know I've tried with Howard. I've given him three boys. I cook. I clean. But nothing ever seems to be enough."

"You'll always be the giver, and Howard is always gonna take." He lit a cigarette, offered Linda one. "How's that for dime-store philosophy?"

Linda and Sam Hugh looked at each other, almost as if they saw each other for the first time. Tears came to their eyes, each showing pity for the other, each understanding that, because of their mother, they had never had a chance for a normal life.

CHAPTER NINE

"I'd like us to walk to the front of the house. If a stranger came, he or she would go to the front door, correct?"

"Yes, a stranger would," Sam Hugh said. "But nobody ever went in that way. I'm certain Mother would never open the front door, even for God himself."

"Okay, let's just start wherever you say."

"The back," Linda said. "Definitely the back."

"I guess I'll turn on a light."

"By the door," Sam Hugh said.

"I want you to look carefully as we go from room to room. I want to know if the furniture's been moved or if anything's missing. We don't want to miss a thing, any clue that might tell us who killed your mother."

"The chair's been moved," Linda said. "Is that the kind of thing we're supposed to look for?"

"Yes, exactly," answered the sheriff.

Linda held tightly to her brother's arm. The lights in all the other rooms were still on. They hesitated and then stepped into the front bedroom, the one where their mother slept. The bed was slightly rumpled, and a green corduroy backrest leaned against the headboard. The lamp on the bedside table cast a circle of light on the books and magazines that lay on the glass top. A pair of reading glasses lay atop the magazines.

"What time did your mother usually go to bed at night?"

"She went to bed late and got up late."

"And was your mother in the habit of making up her bed every morning when she got up?"

"Oh yes, that was almost a compulsion with Mother. She did that before she made her coffee," answered Linda.

The sheriff scribbled on his pad. "Then it would be correct to assume she was reading in bed when she was first disturbed?"

"It certainly appears that way."

Sam Hugh had an uneasy feeling. He knew Sheriff Ball was watching him and thinking he was the murderer, simply because he was gay. He could feel perspiration forming on his upper lip and trickling down under his arms. His hands were wet, and the thirst for whisky was overwhelming.

"Were you always required to keep your room straight, Sam Hugh?"

"Our maid did that. Mother didn't think a man should do 'women's work,'" he said.

Sheriff Ball took one last look to see if he had missed anything in his earlier examination of the bedroom. He saw a brown photo album on a desk and reminded himself to look through the scrapbook later. He knew photo albums often told the true story of family dynamics.

The sheriff patted Linda on the shoulder and said softly, "Okay, we need to go through the rest of the house. It won't be easy for you."

They walked down the dark hall, pausing at each closed bedroom door.

"This was my room," Linda said, pointing at the door being opened by the sheriff. "Oh, no!" she exclaimed, staring at the urine-stained mattress. "Mother should have thrown that away long ago."

The sheriff closed the door quietly. He knew Linda was embarrassed by the sight of her bed.

"Careful," he said. "Don't touch anything. All I want from you is to tell me if you see anything out of place."

Both Linda and Sam Hugh gasped when they saw blood on the bare mattress in the third bedroom.

"We believe your mom was killed here and dragged to the den."

Sam Hugh stopped walking and removed his glasses.

"It's extremely cruel of you to subject us to this. That's our mother's blood on the bed."

"I'm sorry, believe me. Let's walk on through the den and into the kitchen. Just don't look at the floor. Not right now, anyway."

Eager to see the expressions on Linda's and Sam Hugh's faces, the sheriff ushered each in front of him. "See anything out of the ordinary here?"

"These books on the floor . . . that's not normal. And this chair's been moved," Sam Hugh said.

"Yes," Linda said. "Mother was very particular with her books."

The sheriff reached for his notebook again and wrote: *Sam Hugh looks at blood on floor. Linda does not.*

In the kitchen, Sam Hugh sat down at the round maple table. He sighed and said, "Well, there are four chairs around this table. There should be only three. The fourth one belongs over there—under the telephone."

The sheriff opened the refrigerator door and saw a carton of milk, a pitcher of orange juice, and a few other breakfast items.

"Not much food in here."

Sam Hugh said, "Mother didn't like to cook. She brought home chicken, hamburgers, pizza, TV dinners—things like that."

"What about a cleaning lady?

"Josie Walker. She's in the phone book. Her husband's name is Marcus. She wouldn't hurt Mother. She probably didn't like her, though. Mother wasn't friendly with the help."

Linda ignored the conversation and looked out the kitchen window. Heavy black clouds were forming in the southwest.

"Hey, Sam Hugh, I was right." A wide smile crossed her face. "It's going to rain!" she squealed, clapping her hands together. "Oh, I love the rain, I love the rain, I love the rain . . ."

Sam Hugh glanced quickly at the sheriff. "Are we through now?"

"The murderer beat your mother with something heavy and hard. The autopsy will most likely tell us what. We've looked all through the house and out in the yard, but we haven't found the murder weapon yet. That part has me puzzled. I'm also puzzled by the smeared blood on the refrigerator."

Linda began to cry, and Sam Hugh tore off a piece of paper towel from the counter and handed it to her.

"Sheriff Ball," he said in a tone that did not hide his annoyance, "I have no idea who killed my mother. Neither does Linda. I do know that Mother heard a prowler earlier in the summer. She notified the police, or at least she told me she did. I'm sure you could easily check. Perhaps the prowler returned."

He cleared his throat. "Mother had some jewelry, but she kept it down at the bank in a safety deposit box. She wore lots of costume jewelry, but I can't imagine anyone thinking it was valuable. Did you check to see if the silver was still in the buffet?"

Suddenly, Linda covered her mouth with her hand and gagged.

"Can't we get out of here?" she pleaded. "I can smell her blood! I can smell our mother's blood!"

CHAPTER TEN

Linda stood on her brother's front porch, waiting for Howard to come and get her. He had left earlier to get them a motel room, unpack, and take a shower.

A slow, steady rain was beginning to fall. It was getting dark, and lights from the kitchen windows of the surrounding homes were twinkling across Signal Hill.

"All the mothers are trying to figure out what to feed their families," Linda said. The moisture had frizzled her hair, and her brother thought she looked just like she had when he'd first seen her. She was about seven then, her hair parted in the middle and pulled back with hair clasps. She was such a shy little girl. Afraid of her shadow, his mother said many times. It had been a mistake to adopt her, his mother admitted after the first month, but his dad hushed her and told her to make the best of a bad situation.

"I miss my babies, Sam Hugh. I want to get this over with. I want to go home," Linda said between sobs.

"I know you do. They're cute kids. I need to see them more. I'll never have any of my own, but I can be the best uncle they'll ever have."

"Please try," she said, touching his cheek with her dainty hand. "From now on, we'll try to stay in touch better. I do want you to love my children. They need someone to love them unconditionally. Howard expects too much out of them."

"Do you love him, Linda?"

"Does *he* love *me*? That's the sixty-four thousand dollar question."

"I should have told you not to marry him. He wasn't the brightest guy I ever met."

Linda smiled. "Oh, come on, Sam Hugh. Howard was a good catch for me, and you know it."

"He thought our family had money. Wish that was true, don't you?"

"Oh, yes."

"I'm going inside, Linda. I need a drink. Can I fix you something?"

"Oh, no. Maybe some water?"

"Sure," he said. "You aren't getting wet, are you? You can come in if you want to."

"I'm fine. I don't want to make Howard wait a second on me."

"Fuck him."

"Go inside, Sam Hugh. I think I see him now. I'll call you in the morning."

Sam Hugh Park realized, as he watched his sister get into her husband's car, that he was technically an orphan now. He thought back on the days when his dad was alive and gave the noon news radio report from the second floor of his newspaper building. He had once witnessed the robbery of People's Bank on Main Street. In obvious excitement over his good fortune to be able to report a robbery as it actually happened, he'd gotten so worked up that he'd said, "The bank's president is chasing the robbers up the sidewalk. The robbers have stopped and turned around and are pistol whipping Mr. Bryan." Only instead of pistol whipping, he said "whistol pipping."

His father was the quintessential newspaper editor. Everything was about selling papers. He recalled a story Milton Willis, an employee for thirty-five years, loved to tell. Willis had turned in an article that he was especially proud of, but Editor Park said it wasn't controversial enough, and that controversy sold newspapers. A three-inch headline during the Kennedy and Cuban missile crisis exemplified his rule: "Kennedy Castrates Castro." Of course, he later confessed that he was talking about a farmer in Cedarville named Kennedy who castrated his bull named Castro.

He remembered another time when his mother was recovering from an operation at Christmas time, so his dad brought the turkey and dressing into their bedroom. Sam Hugh took those photographs, and he wondered if his mom had saved them. And if she did, where would they be?

He opened the door and went into his house. He needed a drink. He needed many drinks. He had to get the picture of his mother on the den floor out of his head.

"Santos," he said, "fix me a whiskey, a strong one, and be quick about it."

CHAPTER ELEVEN

Monday, May eighteenth, dawned brightly beautiful—the way early summer days arrive after a good rain. The grass was greener, the sky bluer, the clouds a soft peach. Spring had arrived late that year, which made the scent of honeysuckle seem even sweeter as it wafted across the barbed wire fences separating one rural property from the other. In the older part of town, where two-storied houses once represented the socially prominent, lavender blossoms hung like clusters of grapes from the wisteria vines that traveled up sides of houses and across porch roofs. Rose gardens celebrated summer with sweet scents from roses with names like Silver Moon, Simplicity, and Moonlight Melody.

This first day of the school week was not like other Monday mornings or the ones to follow. News of Ruie Ann Park's death had been reported on Channel 5 out of Fort Smith on the evening news and on the front pages of the *Southwest Times Record* and *The Arkansas Gazette*, the Little Rock morning newspaper. School children, anxious for school to be over for the summer, heard their parents talking and became frightened, using that as a reason to stay home. A steady line of cars and trucks drove up and down Log Town Hill, slowing in front of the house that was referred to by many as the showplace of Van Buren.

Rusty and Linda Myers dropped their children off at school and drove to Sam Hugh's home. When they knocked on the door, a friend of theirs, Martha Robinson, opened the door. She welcomed them in with a plea.

"Maybe you can convince Sam Hugh to get in the shower. He's so drunk, he's not making sense."

Santos had stayed the night, dozing in the chair. He nodded to Linda Myers and shook Rusty's hand.

"He's in bad shape. Drank all night long," Santos said. "Never left that chair except to take a piss, and I don't think he always did that when he should have. His clothes are wet. So is the chair."

Rusty took Sam Hugh's arm and pulled with all his strength.

"Sam Hugh, come on, friend, and get in the shower."

"I'm drunk, Rusty." His words were mumbled and disconnected, not unlike other words during other drunks when Rusty had put Sam Hugh to bed. He remembered the two-week drunk he'd gone on after he got the appointment to be a federal prosecutor. Rusty had taken care of him that time by making excuses to the federal judge he was assigned to.

"Mother's dead, dead, dead. I keep seeing her on the floor."

"Listen, Sam Hugh. You've got to sober up. Santos told me you're supposed to go see Sheriff Ball this morning. You've got to sober up."

Rusty nodded to Santos. "Get his other arm, and let's drag him to the shower if we have to."

Martha, a feisty woman popular in local Democratic politics, had worked hard in Bill Clinton's race for governor of Arkansas, as had Sam Hugh. In fact, an autographed picture of Clinton hung over his desk in his office.

Linda Myers turned to Martha, who was busy searching for something in her bag.

"I'm going over to clean up all the blood in the house. I told Rusty I'd do it. Want to help me?"

Martha took the top off the lipstick she was searching for and said, "Oh, I couldn't. I faint at the sight of blood." She ran the tube over her lips and rubbed them together. "Besides, I have to get home."

Not surprised that Martha wouldn't want to help, she told her it was okay, that she had brought rubber gloves, a bucket, and some old towels from home.

Linda Myers was a petite woman with short, auburn hair and a smattering of freckles across her face. As a faithful member of the First Presbyterian Church and homeroom mother for three separate classes, her life was busy. She worked in the office of a pediatrician in Fort Smith. Her husband was in charge of a government office dedicated to bringing new businesses into the area. Both were active in theatre groups. They seemed to be a happily married couple, and with the passage of time, year after year, their children counted themselves lucky that their parents loved each other.

Chief Hicks sat in a chair by the back door. He was finishing up the last of two sausage biscuits he'd bought from the McDonald's down the hill.

"Good morning, Mrs. Myers." He noticed her bucket was full of cleaning supplies. "Before you start cleaning, I need to check with the sheriff to see if it's okay."

"My husband spoke with Sheriff Ball earlier this morning. He said it was fine."

"Well, I can't just take your word for it. Let me call the sheriff."

Linda Myers took a deep breath. She had not slept much the night before, and she wanted to get at the job before she lost her courage.

"Okay, then."

While she waited for permission to get down on her hands and knees to scrub blood off the floor, she walked along the back patio, remembering the wedding held for Linda and Howard in the backyard. It had been in early August, and she remembered how hot it was. Candles in hurricane lamps had lined the driveway, and during the ceremony, you could hear the glass break from the heat of the candles combined with the 100 degrees of the day.

Glenda Yancy, a darling little girl of eight who lived across the street, had worn a blue dotted Swiss dress and acted as flower girl. Perhaps she had been Linda's only real friend, and she had doted on the little girl, always giving her presents for her birthdays.

Howard was from North Little Rock, and he'd had more guests seated on his side than Linda had had on hers. She and Rusty had been there, and she remembered the shy, almost frightened look on the bride's face. Her brother had given her away to a man Rusty and his wife had taken an immediate dislike to, and they'd both confided later that they didn't think the marriage would last more than a year or two. Linda Myers also remembered the sour expression on Ruie Ann's face, like she had smelled a foul odor. Her hair had been tightly permed, and she had worn a navy blue dress with a white collar that Linda had bought her for the wedding. She remembered how proud Linda had been that she was also able to buy her mother a dress for the rehearsal dinner held at Lewis Cafeteria in Fort Smith. By then, the father of the bride was dead.

Linda Myers snapped back to the horrid scene of the murder when she heard Chief Hicks lumbering across the graveled drive.

"Sheriff Ball says you can go on in. Mrs. Park's daughter is inside. You should tell her what you're going to do. She's pretty jumpy."

Linda Myers heard Linda in her mother's bedroom. The door was slightly ajar, so she knocked a few times.

"It's me, Linda Myers."

Linda stood at her mother's chest of drawers. She held a white nylon slip in her hand.

"The funeral director told me to pick out the clothes Mother should be buried in."

"Oh, okay. I only wanted to tell you that I'll be in the den, cleaning up."

Linda lowered her head and murmured a thank you.

"It's hard. Going through her stuff, I mean."

"I'm sure. I'll just get along with my business."

Linda Myers first walked into the bedroom where the bloody mattress lay atop a maple bed. She attempted to turn it over, but it was too heavy. Instead, she leaned it up between the wall and the side of the bed.

She dropped a large sponge into the soapy water she'd prepared in the Park kitchen sink. Another bucket of rinse water held an old cloth diaper. On her hands and knees, she followed the dried bloody trail into the den, scrubbing and rinsing, scrubbing and rinsing, scrubbing and rinsing until the water had to be dumped down the kitchen sink. She repeated the process until she reached the den where Sam Hugh had found his mother. Quickly realizing the blood was too heavy and thick for a sponge, she went into the kitchen and found a spatula.

When she finished, she took the two buckets and threw them in an outside garbage can. For a moment, she wondered if some kind of important evidence might be in the can, but she couldn't bring herself to look and prolong her stay. *Enough for friendship*, she thought. *Enough for love.*

When she left, she noticed a bloody palm print on the refrigerator door. She wondered if she should wipe it off, thinking surely the police had already seen it and taken prints. Surely, they had. She left it, just in case.

The cleaning job had nauseated Linda Myers. She needed to find Rusty to take her home. She didn't think she could stay around this gruesome scene another minute.

She would never have imagined herself involved so intimately with a murder. She was an Air Force brat, and she'd lived all over, so when she met Rusty at the University of Arkansas and married the man who wanted to settle down in Van Buren, a town he was born in, she was excited about establishing roots. Sam Hugh Park had welcomed her, and she was charmed by his intellect and his ability to see humor in the most mundane of events.

Sam Hugh could tell of a trip to Sherman's Grocery Store, where a variety of customers came down from the small surrounding communities of Figure Five, Natural Dam, Chester, and Mountainburg for their Saturday shopping, forming the heart of a great story, and told with a masterful talent for colorful description and perfect impersonations of the people he called "genuine."

Like Holden Caulfield, Sam Hugh's favorite literary character, he could spot a phony a block away. Even the car he currently drove was the object of a good tale. He'd taken it in when a client couldn't pay a fee, and the hood had come off on the Arkansas River Bridge.

"Did I go back to get it? Hell, no. I could have been arrested for causing an accident."

Linda Myers also recalled the young woman Sam Hugh had dated in college, a journalism major who could match wits with him. She wanted to marry him, but Ruie Ann discouraged their friendship. Eventually, they stopped seeing each other. Was Ruie Ann Park jealous of all women where her son was concerned? Did she condone the young boys with whom he had sexual relationships as just fun and games and nothing more? As long as Sam Hugh was without a wife, he would forever be tied to his mother in a man-woman relationship. It wasn't unheard of. Shakespeare had written plays about just that sort of thing.

Linda Myers walked toward their car and stood against the side door. It felt warm on her back. She was in such a hurry to complete her task that she hadn't noticed the steady ache between her shoulders and lower back.

She saw Linda emerge from the kitchen door, carrying a paper sack and shoe box in one hand and a garment bag in the other. She barely smiled as she walked by, and Linda Myers thought about the old adage of trying to get through an unpleasant task by taking one step at a time. That's what they all would have to do.

CHAPTER TWELVE

By Monday afternoon, the murder investigation was in full swing. Don Taylor with the state police called in Richard Earl McCracken for an interview at the Van Buren Police Department. They sat across from each other at a small wooden desk, sticky with deposits of grime that came from the many hands of men—and a few women—who had been questioned there before.

McCracken was Sam Hugh's secretary-bookkeeper. He stated that on the previous Friday he had gone to lunch in Fort Smith at the Town Club with Sam Hugh and Ralph Ballentine, a banker from Alma. They then looked at a business Ballentine was remodeling and after that went to the Greyhound Bus Station to pick up Ruie Ann Park, who was returning from a research trip to Cincinnati. Her bus was late, so they met Rusty Myers at the Stephens Building and visited with him. After that, they went back to the bus station, picked up Ruie Ann, and brought her home to Fayetteville Street.

"Were Sam Hugh and his mother happy to see each other?" Taylor asked.

"Of course they were happy to see each other. For about a minute, and then she started in on him, but that was normal."

Richard McCracken was a charming fellow whose sexual preferences were easily recognized. A nice enough looking young man of thirty, he lived in a small hamlet named Dora, barely in the state of Arkansas and just a breath away from Oklahoma. He was one of those people who like to be in the know.

"Ruie Ann told me about three weeks ago she was going to renew a CD that matured. It was going to Linda, and she told me she changed her will six months earlier."

Taylor could see the gleeful expression on McCracken's face.

"You must have really been a good friend of Mrs. Park for her to tell you about her financial business."

"Oh, yes, we had a remarkable friendship."

"And when did you see Sam Hugh again? I mean, after the Friday at the bus stop?"

"Let's see now. I went to Rusty and Linda's house for dinner, and Sam Hugh was there."

"Is that Rusty and Linda Myers? He was a business partner of Sam Hugh's, wasn't he? Did they have something cooking? Something that required a hefty investment?"

"Oh, yes. Myers. They were always plotting a way to get rich. But that night we just had dinner, and Sam Hugh left early to go watch a movie on cable. I stayed and visited until ten or eleven."

"Do you remember what Sam Hugh was wearing that Saturday night?"

"Slacks, loafers, yellow sweater."

Detective Taylor leaned closer to McCracken. He could smell his bad breath—a mixture of coffee, cigarettes, and last night's beer—but he didn't back off.

"And how did you find out about the murder?"

"Cathy Gifford called me Sunday afternoon and told me to get up to Sam Hugh's. She was crying real hard, so I knew something was bad. I didn't know what had happened until I got there."

"And who told you?"

"Sam Hugh said his mom was murdered. And he said the police thought he did it."

"And do *you* think he did it?"

"I don't know. All I know is that I'm scared to death. I could be next."

"And why are you in danger?" He watched as Richard McCracken twisted the rings on his left hand, and Taylor noticed his nails were polished a light mauve. It was hard for Taylor to hide his disgust.

"Who'd want to kill you?"

McCracken's lips quivered, and he cleared his throat, stifling a sob.

"I know a lot about a lot of things, Detective Taylor. I know Sam Hugh owes a lot of money to a lot of people. He probably wouldn't want me to tell everything I know."

"Do you think Sam Hugh is capable of killing his mother?"

McCracken looked at his watch and then back at Taylor.

"I'm supposed to help Sam Hugh pick out a casket down at Ocker's Funeral Home."

"I repeat the question. Was Sam Hugh Park capable of murdering his mother?"

"I don't know, Detective. I honestly don't know."

Taylor pushed a white tablet and pen toward McCracken.

"I want you to give me a list of the men who wandered in and out of Sam Hugh's home. I want to talk to them."

McCracken hesitated a moment before he picked up the pen. He looked at his watch again, to buy some time. He didn't know if he was going to write down the name of a killer or killers.

"Do it," Taylor ordered.

Richard quickly wrote down the names:

1. Santos
2. Mark Mullins

3. Gary Shoop
4. Mitchell Domer
5. Dennis Whisenant
6. Tracey Strickland
7. Rick Lewis
8. Chuck Cox
9. Ricky Havens

CHAPTER THIRTEEN

Ruie Ann Park's funeral was held at Ocker Memorial Chapel in Van Buren at three p.m. on Friday, May twenty-second. There was a big crowd, including Sam Hugh and Linda, who both sobbed during the service.

The Van Buren *Press Argus* and the *Southwest Times Record* printed obituaries with Ruie's long list of accomplishments. She was a member of a pioneer Arkansas family. She was a retired schoolteacher and a noted historian. She was a former co-owner of *The Press Argus*. She was the founder of the Van Buren Garden Club and the Crawford County Historical Association. She was a member of the Van Buren Historic District Commission and the Women's Literary Guild. She was a member of the General Society of Mayflower Descendants of America, Daughters of the American Revolution, and the Pilgrim John Howland Society.

Memorials were established with the Women's Literary Club in Van Buren. And, as her daughter requested, there was a memorial fund for the Cabot Library building fund.

She was buried at Gracelawn Cemetery in Van Buren next to her daughter, who was born in 1932 but only lived a day. And didn't have a name.

After the funeral, two classmates of Linda and Sam Hugh, Nancy Baker and Joyce Ann Patton, met at the Cottage Café for coffee and pie. Nancy, a junior high teacher—known throughout the school system as a teacher who demanded and received complete attention from her students—lived in Fort Smith and was the wife of the mayor. She still kept up with her fellow high school cheerleader and friend, Joyce Ann.

Joyce Ann worked in Fort Smith for Arkansas Best Corporation, but she still lived in Van Buren. She excelled at her job, and she actually earned a larger paycheck than her husband. An only child, she doted on her parents and had built a home for them on rural property her family owned.

Nancy stirred sugar into her coffee and then tasted the first bite of her coconut pie.

"Did you notice how thin Linda is?"

"Yeah, but she's always been thin."

Joyce Ann felt a little guilty eating her chocolate pie in the middle of the day. Their booth sat against a plate-glass window and offered a closeup view of the shoppers on Main Street.

Business along Main Street had recently improved. Tax incentives for investing in the restoration of historical districts had enticed antique dealers, interior decorators, artists, and restaurateurs to settle on Main Street. The old train station had been converted to a welcome center and offered excursion train rides. During the spring and fall, when the Ozark and Boston Mountains were at their peak of beauty, passengers could ride to and from Fayetteville, the home of the University of Arkansas.

Joyce Ann brushed through her short, brown hair with her fingertips and took the first bite of her pie.

"Did you see how Sam Hugh kept his arm around Linda all through the service?"

"And how detached her husband acted," Nancy said. "Big shot Howard."

Joyce Ann remembered their high school ten-year reunion, when she and her husband had tried their best to keep a conversation going with Linda and Howard.

"Poor Linda. I think she might have jumped from the frying pan into the fire."

Nancy laughed, remembering that Joyce Ann had always been full of old sayings she'd learned from her father, a man who could charm anyone into buying insurance.

"You know, I remember when Linda was adopted. My mother said Sam Hugh had actually picked her out. Like a Christmas present."

Joyce Ann looked up and saw several people she'd seen at the funeral and nodded a hello.

"I remember her playing on the monkey bars. In her own little world. The bell rang, and all the rest of us ran inside. But not Linda. Mrs. Gray had to go outside and tell her that recess was over. She had to do that a lot of times."

"I remember when Ruie Ann taught eighth grade history, and I took up the absentee lists. She had a ton of pictures around her desk. And they were all of Sam Hugh. None of Linda."

"Oh, yeah, she doted on him. He could do no wrong. She's the reason he was . . . you know."

"When the Parks lived two doors down from us, before they built that mansion on the hill, Linda and I walked home from school together. She told me she wished she could live with my family. And one time, when we were in the sixth grade, she started her period at school. Poor little Linda, she didn't know what had happened, so the teacher asked me to walk home with her so she could change her clothes. Well, when we got there, Ruie Ann shouted at Linda and told her she was going to have to learn to take care of herself. That she shouldn't leave the school grounds under any condition. Even if her silly teacher told her to."

"Oh, how awful."

"Yeah, I thought so, too. If my mom had treated me that way, well, I don't know what I would have done."

Joyce Ann leaned closer to Nancy and whispered, "I really hate to say this, but Ruie Ann deserved what happened to her."

Nancy shook her head. "Nobody deserves to die like she did. I heard her head was bashed in with a fireplace poker."

"You do know Wayne Hicks is telling everybody Sam Hugh killed his mom."

"Wayne Hicks should keep his mouth shut. Just because Sam Hugh is a homosexual doesn't automatically make him a murderer. He loved his mother, and God knows, she loved him."

"Remember when he got to be a page in Washington?" Joyce Ann said. "And she moved up there with him?"

"Remember he was the master of ceremonies at that dance show on television?"

"Oh, he was smart," Joyce Ann said, counting on her fingers. "National Merit Scholar, US prosecuting attorney. He could have done anything he wanted to do, but his mother ruined him. I know they say that homosexuals are born that way, but she sure helped him along. I think that's why he drank so much."

"But who killed her?" Nancy asked. "Maybe it *was* Sam Hugh, but I don't think so."

"Could have been one of his friends," Joyce Ann said. "I heard he got most of them out of jails."

"I bet she left Sam Hugh everything and Linda nothing."

The two women finished their pie and promised to see each other more often. They had no idea they would soon be attending another Park funeral.

CHAPTER FOURTEEN

On the fifth of June, Don Taylor paid another call to Sam Hugh Park. He planned to catch him unawares. But when he arrived, he discovered Sam Hugh was gone.

Richard McCracken stood up from behind his desk, clearly agitated by the policeman's visit.

"Sam Hugh is on vacation in Salt Lake City. He and Gary Shoop went up there to visit a friend who's in the hospital."

"When is he scheduled to return?"

"This coming Thursday. He said there was nothing wrong with him leaving the state. He said he hadn't been charged with anything. That's right, isn't it? You're not here to arrest me for taking him to the airport?"

Taylor let out a long sigh that did not hide his exasperation.

"No, I'm only here to follow up on our last interview. What can you tell me about Sam Hugh's law practice? Was it successful? Was he making money?"

McCracken told him that Sam Hugh's collections were down, and that he owed somewhere between $45,000 and $65,000 to two different banks.

"He also has a few hot checks out."

Taylor raised his eyebrows. "That's interesting. Go on." He'd been around McCracken enough to know that he couldn't keep from telling things he knew he shouldn't.

"Sam Hugh told me before his mother went on her trip that he was going to ask her for help. I don't know if he did or not. Maybe he decided to wait until she got back."

Taylor smiled and winked. "Maybe he did ask her, and she said no."

"I have no idea, and that's the truth."

Taylor thought he was going to hit the jackpot with McCracken.

"I understand Sam Hugh has moved into his mother's home. Did he take all his boys with him?"

"I'm not sure. This has me so upset. I don't know if my life is in danger or not. I do feel safer knowing that Sam Hugh is gone for now."

"Does Sam Hugh know the way you feel?" asked Taylor.

McCracken began to sob. "Of course he doesn't. And please, I beg of you, don't tell him. I need this job. I have bills to pay. He's got just enough in his office account to keep me on for two months. Do you know how hard it is to get a job these days?"

Taylor nodded. "We want you to take a polygraph test."

McCracken sobbed louder. "Do you think I killed Ruie Ann? I didn't. I swear to God. I was home asleep when she was killed."

"We're investigating everyone connected to this case in any way, shape, or form. I don't know who is guilty, but I'm sure as hell going to find out. If you know anything, you'd better tell me."

"I apologize for crying," he said, reaching for a Kleenex and pulling it dramatically out of the box. "This has got me so upset. I can't sleep at night. I've asked the doctor for something for my nerves."

"You be at the Van Buren Police Station tomorrow at two o'clock. Investigator W.B. Baskin will administer the test."

Taylor said good-bye and left the office. He climbed into his police car, but before he turned on the ignition, he lit a cigarette. He smiled, knowing that Richard McCracken would not get a good night's sleep tonight. McCracken was going to help him nail Sam Hugh Park for his mother's death. He had killed her, and it was only a matter of time until he or one of his queer buddies told him so.

McCracken watched out the window as Taylor finally backed out and drove away. He took a silver flask out of his desk drawer. The flask was a gift from a pharmacist in Conway before he was sent to prison for filling too many phony prescriptions. That had been a sweet time in McCracken's life. He had a nice little apartment on Rebsamen Park Road in Little Rock, a membership to Gold's Gym, and a tidy allowance. He was only twenty-five then, and he often posed for gay men's magazines. But that was then, and now he lived in a trailer and might be murdered before the day was over. He began to sob again. He didn't deserve this. He didn't deserve this at all.

He put the flask to his mouth but was astonished to find it empty. He threw it back into the drawer and cried some more.

The phone didn't ring for the rest of the afternoon. Nobody wanted a lawyer who might have killed his mother. He knew Sam Hugh's visit to a sick friend was an excuse for going on a bender. Hell, Sam Hugh was drunk when he got on the plane. He was surprised the guy at the counter sold him a ticket.

That night, at home in his trailer, Richard plotted out what he would say the next day at the police station. If Sam Hugh didn't kill his mother, then who did? They fought all the time, but then they always made up. Sam Hugh could say cruel things when he was drunk, but the next day he always apologized. He probably picked up a poker and hit her because she wouldn't give him any more money. Yes, while Sam Hugh is gone, he'll tell that Mr. Baskin fellow what he really thinks happened. It never hurts to get in good with the police.

Before he went to sleep, he called Rusty Myers.

"Hey, Rusty, I just need someone to talk to. Do you have a minute?"

Rusty and Linda Myers had been working in their backyard on Seventh Circle, which was located up a hill, northwest from the Park house.

"What's the matter? Has something happened to Sam Hugh?"

"Oh, no, I'm feeling a little scared. That Taylor guy wants me to come in for a lie detector test."

Rusty sighed, relieved he didn't have to leave his house and bail Sam Hugh out of some mess.

"That guy has been dogging me, too. He thinks Sam Hugh and I were involved in some business scheme, and Sam Hugh killed his mother to get money for the investment. Hell, you know how Sam Hugh and I were always talking about this property or that property. Taylor showed up on our doorstep minutes before we were to leave for Ruie's funeral. He told me he'd taken a bunch of psychology courses, and it was a fact that homosexuals had a love-hate relationship with their mother. He's a jerk. Don't worry. Just go down and tell the truth as you understand it. You can do that, can't you, Richard?"

CHAPTER FIFTEEN

Chief Hicks had a hard time keeping his mouth shut while investigating the case. At the Cottage Café, where a few women and a lot of men gathered for breakfast, Hicks held a captive audience, something that seldom happened in his life. He enjoyed being the one who knew something nobody else did.

"You should have seen the murder scene. Bloody as hell. Sam Hugh had plenty of time to get rid of evidence. His mom was killed around one or two in the morning, and he didn't report her dead until almost two the next afternoon. It doesn't take a genius to figure who killed who."

P.D. DuVall, a Van Buren graduate with a master's degree and an officer in the Arkansas Air National Guard, defended Sam Hugh.

"Are you calling yourself a genius?"

Other men sitting around the table laughed.

"Just because he lives across the street from his mom and found the body doesn't automatically make him guilty, for Christ's sake." DuVall motioned to the waitress for a warm-up and lit his third cigarette of the day. "You want to condemn the guy because he's gay.

Smart and gay is a lethal combination, according to you and a lot of folks around here. You're all a bunch of idiots."

Carl Creekmore, a local attorney with an IQ that equaled DuVall's and who had outsmarted most of the men in town, agreed.

"Hicks, you need to shut up this talk about Sam Hugh killing his mom. He's innocent until proven guilty." He winked at DuVall. "You have heard of that, haven't you?"

But Creekmore and DuVall were outnumbered. If a straw vote was taken in every church in Van Buren on any given Sunday, the results would find Sam Hugh Park guilty. He was a homosexual, and that was against God's law, and, therefore, he was guilty.

Sam Hugh knew nearly everyone in town thought he was a murderer. The harassment by the police continued throughout the summer and into the fall of 1981. His gay friends were repeatedly called in for more interviews. A few of them actually told the police that Sam Hugh had admitted to killing his mom when he was drunk, which was most of the time. Lie detector tests were given several times to Sam Hugh. On one finding, an Arkansas state police polygraph examiner concluded that Mr. Sam Hugh Park "intentionally tried to defeat the administration of an effective polygraph examination . . . in his trade as a lawyer, and his continuing movement, even after instructions, which makes it impossible for this examiner to render anything but inconclusive."

In other words, because Sam Hugh was a lawyer, he was able to outsmart a polygraph test.

Rusty and Linda Myers remained steadfast friends. They knew how hard Ruie Ann's death had affected her son. On some days, he was inconsolable. They visited with Sam Hugh often, either at the Winter Palace, where he now lived with a steady flow of people in and out, or in the Myers' shady backyard filled with white and red impatiens, several varieties of hostas, and hanging baskets of petunias and ferns. Their yard was a respite for Sam Hugh, and even though his friends tried to steer the conversations away from his mother's death, it always hung over them like a heavy cloud.

"What if I did kill her?" Sam Hugh asked one pleasant evening a year or so after his mother's death. Rusty had grilled steaks, and they had finished the last of a peach cobbler. "What if I had a blackout and killed her and just don't remember?"

"Don't be ridiculous, Sam Hugh. You loved your mom, and you always did a good job of patronizing her with your 'Now, Mother' and 'You're absolutely right, Mother.'"

Rusty's compassion for his Acacia fraternity brother was genuine. He had always admired the way Sam Hugh dealt with his mother from the time he reached the age to understand that Ruie Ann Park was a woman who needed to be handled diplomatically. Not everyone in Van Buren was willing to tolerate her bossiness, and not everyone was impressed by her claim of being descended from not one, but two people who came over on the Mayflower.

Sam Hugh stood up from the black wrought-iron table they sat around. He arched his back and rubbed his shoulders and sat back down again. He'd only eaten a bite or two of his steak and had declined the cobbler because he said he was watching his weight.

"Oh, you're right," Sam Hugh said. "I know that. I was thinking about how Mother drove. We'd be on our way to Fayetteville on that treacherous 71 highway, and she'd drive thirty on the flat stretches and fifty on the curves."

Rusty and Linda Myers laughed. Sam Hugh was a great storyteller, and when he was only a little drunk, there was no better comic around. They especially liked to hear Sam Hugh tell about his courtroom antics. He once defended a young man named Billy Bob something. When the judge asked Billy Bob something to rise and face the court, Sam Hugh interrupted the judge and said, very flamboyantly, "Your honor, my client prefers the name *Rolando*."

Linda Myers had especially loved her visits to the Park home when she and Rusty were first married. The home was a showplace with its pecan wood flooring, expensive rugs, and genuine antiques from the Federalist period that Ruie Ann loved. One rug came from New Orleans and was woven especially to celebrate the bicentennial anniversary in 1976. Often when they visited, Sam Hugh played the piano for them. He was a great musician, and Linda Myers loved to hear him play—classical, romantic ballads, show tunes. Sam Hugh had perfect pitch.

But as more and more undesirable folks camped out in the Winter Palace, Linda Myers decided her visits with Sam Hugh would only continue at their house. On her last time to drop in on Sam Hugh, with her young son in tow, she was invited in by a man she had never seen before. He was wearing red tennis shoes and a red patent leather belt with his name, *Timothy*, engraved on the back. He said he and his mother were sleeping in the guest room, but she hadn't awakened yet.

Sam Hugh's law practice suffered because he didn't take care of the cases he had, and no new ones were coming in. More and more, he spent money on lavish trips to San Francisco, in which he paid airfare and hotel arrangements for some of the same men who had told the police they thought he had killed his mother.

Even though he inherited enough to live on comfortably, Sam Hugh squandered the money and was forced to sell items out of his mother's house. He and one of his buddies took all the silver and china over to Tulsa to sell to an antique dealer. After that came the expensive rugs, the antique furniture, and the portraits of dead officers of the American Revolution.

Sam Hugh was often seen walking down Main Street, a glass in one hand and a bottle in the other. He particularly liked to visit with Garrick Feldman, mainly because Feldman now owned *The Press Argus*, which Hugh Sam's parents had owned for fifty years. He felt safe there in the building he had run around in as a boy, watching the mysterious printing press perform its duties. Feldman enjoyed hearing stories about the first days of the newspaper when Hugh Park put out the paper single-handedly.

But he did not enjoy Sam Hugh when he stank of vomit and piss. And there was nothing entertaining about witnessing the steady, debilitating decline of a once brilliant mind.

Tiny broken blood vessels appeared on Sam Hugh's cheeks and nose, and his shoulders narrowed and sagged into a bloated and distended stomach. Food didn't taste good to him, so he didn't eat. He smoked and drank until he passed out, and when he awoke, he started the process all over again. He couldn't drive a car because his hands shook uncontrollably, so Bill Spradley made an every-other-day delivery of Ancient Age in a half-gallon bottle.

CHAPTER SIXTEEN

One morning in early October, Rusty received a call from Kay Lynn, a childhood friend of Sam Hugh's.

"Rusty, this is Kay. I'm calling for your help. Because I'm a social worker, people think I can do something to make Sam Hugh stop drinking. I've had three calls this past week, and people are telling me that Sam Hugh is wearing dirty clothes with food stains down the front. He's walking down the sidewalks drunk as a skunk."

Rusty sighed. "All that's true, I'm afraid. How can I help you?"

"Do me a favor. Call Sam Hugh and tell him we'd like to see him. You have to go with me and give me moral support."

"I'll do it."

Later in the week, Rusty called Kay.

"It's a go for Saturday."

They got to the Winter Palace about ten in the morning and were ushered into the kitchen by a scruffy teenage boy with a greasy Elvis Presley hairdo. Sam Hugh sat at a round kitchen table, a fifth of bourbon and a water glass filled with ice in front of him. He wore a dingy white undershirt and pajama bottoms. With a gracious welcome and a sweep of his arm, he invited them to sit down.

"Doesn't Kay look great, Rusty? She looks even better than she did in high school."

Rusty blushed, and Kay thanked him for the compliment.

Kay was a pretty woman. Tall and thin, with black hair and green eyes, she had a no-nonsense presence about her. Those who ever crossed her were sorry they did.

"That was then, and this is now," Kay said. "It's now, and we're here to talk about you."

Sam Hugh poured some bourbon over the ice.

"You look great, and you haven't mellowed at all with time. You're still scary and dictatorial."

Another sleazy-looking boy came in with an offer of coffee, and Kay and Rusty accepted. Elvis served it up, and both boys swished around, pretending to clean the countertops.

"You two may leave," Sam Hugh said. "Now."

Both boys left, but it was clear they wanted to stay.

Sam Hugh sipped his whiskey.

"High school. It seems so long ago and yet like yesterday. Rusty, Kay used to scare me sometimes. When we worked together on the yearbook, we were allowed to use the school car to solicit paid advertising. One day, she and I signed for the car, but it turned out she had no intention of selling ads. She decided we should drive up Highway 71 to Mount Gaylor and climb that old wooden tower, and said we'd be back to school in plenty of time." He chuckled and began again the story of their high school days. "I protested and told her to let me out immediately, but she kept driving at a high speed all the way to Mount Gaylor. She climbed the tower while I cowered in the car, feeling sure we'd both end up expelled from school or in a bad wreck."

"I don't remember that," Kay said. "Enough of the high school stuff. It's brass tacks time. You're an alcoholic, Sam Hugh. You must know that. But you can get sober, get well. You must feel like hell most of the time. You sure look like hell and smell like hell. You're already a little jaundiced."

"And remember the time—"

Kay interrupted. "You're an addict. You can't shake the booze by yourself. Let me get you some help. There are treatment centers, halfway houses, places where you can sober up and get healthy. I can help with that. Please, please let me."

"And I'll drive you anywhere you choose," Rusty said.

Sam Hugh didn't even look at Rusty. "And that time on the band bus—"

"Hush," Kay said. "Don't you want to get off this treadmill? Feel good again? Be *you* again? This stuff is killing you fast."

Sam Hugh took a longer drink of whiskey.

"Okay," Kay said. "If you tell me you don't want to stop drinking and you intend to die like this—and soon—then I'll leave you alone."

Sam Hugh reached across the table and took Kay's hands in his.

"I haven't the least desire to stop drinking, and I intend to die like this. And soon."

Kay and Rusty said their good-byes and left. The next time they would see him would be when they sat next to him as he lay dying on a hospital bed.

Ruie Ann directing one of the many elaborate
birthday parties she held for Sam Hugh

**Linda, Hugh (Dad),
and Sam Hugh**

**Linda, Ruie Ann, and
Sam Hugh on Easter Sunday**

The young Sam Hugh

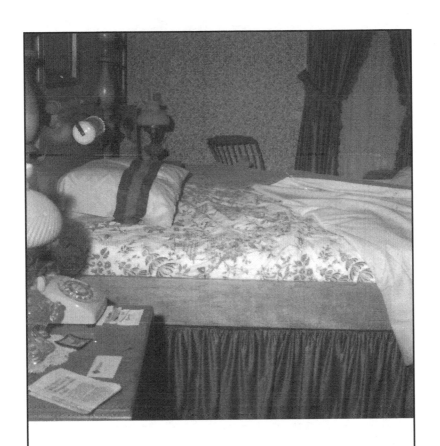

Ruie Ann's bedroom

CHAPTER SEVENTEEN

Sam Hugh Park was drunk the entire month of December, 1982, and while his accusers celebrated New Year's Day with black-eyed peas and football games, he began throwing up blood. Richard McCracken took him to the emergency room at a Fort Smith hospital, where he was admitted. His longtime friends from high school heard about him being hospitalized and set up schedules for sitting with him. Remembering the Sam Hugh of journalism class or the band or the student council or the Latin club, they were shocked to see their friend with his stomach as distended as any eight-month-pregnant woman and his skin the color of a ripe cantaloupe.

Kay Lynn was one of the friends who came to sit with Sam Hugh. Bloody tissues littered the floor, and it was obvious to Kay that Sam Hugh needed oxygen and an IV going to keep him hydrated. Never one to avoid confrontation, Kay stormed to the nursing station and slapped her hand flat on the desk.

"Mr. Park is not getting proper care."

"Room number?" the nurse said without looking up.

"It's down the hall on your right. Room 513 or 514. I'm not really sure—something like that. His lips are chapped and bleeding. I want you to call the attending physician right now. He needs an IV, and he needs oxygen, and he needs some of those moisture wipes to keep his lips moist!"

In a matter of minutes, two nurses and a member of housekeeping were in his room. Kay stood back, supervising with her green eyes, pleased with herself. Sam Hugh Park had been dismissed as some drunk who was going to die anyway, but she had taken care to see that he at least died as comfortably as possible.

Kay opened the blinds to let in some light and stood looking out on the street below. It was spitting snow, and she could tell by the way people were huddled up in their coats and walking briskly that the wind was blowing. She heard a soft knock on the door, and she went to answer it. Linda Martin and her husband, Howard, stood outside. Neither seemed eager to enter the room.

Kay patted Linda's shoulder. She had been in a dance class with Linda when they were children, and they had graduated from high school in the same class of 1959.

"He looks real bad," she said, "so be prepared."

Linda whispered, "Is he awake?"

"Oh, no."

Linda walked over to her brother's bed. She put her hands to her face.

"Oh, God, oh, God, oh, my God."

Kay looked across the room at Howard, who stood smugly against the wall. He made no move to console his wife or pay his respects to his dying brother-in-law.

Linda took Kay's arm.

"When I told the nurse outside that I was Sam Hugh's sister and his next of kin, she said they had no record of any living relatives."

Kay saw the hurt in Linda's eyes.

"Oh, it was just a clerical error. Don't be offended."

"Oh, Kay, you know that's not right. Sam Hugh didn't want anyone to know I was his sister. He's always been a little ashamed of me. When we were at the student union in college, he'd pretend he didn't see me."

Kay remembered when she and both Park children were in dance classes when they were about eleven or twelve. Sam Hugh was a wonderful little dancer, but Linda was not. Ruie Ann made fun of her in front of everybody.

"Come, let's look out the window and see if it's snowing," Kay said.

The classmates stood side by side at the window and watched snowflakes fall, as gentle as tears.

CHAPTER EIGHTEEN

Sam Hugh Park died on January seventeenth, 1983. He was forty years old.

News of his death reached Rusty and Linda Myers via a telephone call from Richard McCracken.

"He's gone," he said.

Linda Myers drew a deep breath and motioned for Rusty to come to the phone.

"It's Sam Hugh," she whispered. "He died just a few minutes ago."

Rusty shook his head. He was in no condition to talk. He'd known the phone call was coming, but he didn't want to acknowledge his friend's death. Not right now, anyway. Instead, he walked out to his front yard, a showplace in the spring and summer, but on this January day, with week-old snow lying on the frozen earth, it closely resembled the way his heart felt.

News of Sam Hugh's death spread quickly. Fellow classmates, some who had not yet reached the age of forty, the age at which life should be at its zenith of good health and good jobs, began to question their own mortality.

"Wow," more than a few said. "You really can kill yourself by drinking too much."

Others thought he'd gotten just what he deserved for killing his own mother.

And the young men, the ones who had leeched off Sam Hugh Park, began to wonder where their next case of beer would come from.

But those who loved Sam Hugh Park grieved his passing and paid tribute to him at the Ocker Funeral Home on the following Wednesday afternoon. His body was buried next to his mother's at Gracelawn Cemetery.

When *The Press Argus* came out that week, the editorial by Garrick Feldman was devoted to Sam Hugh Park. It made police officers and more than a few stalwart citizens squirm because it chastised those who had viciously branded him a murderer but were unable to prove it.

"The police never did make an arrest in the case," Feldman wrote. "At first they sounded confident about getting the killer, but as the days and weeks and months wore on, no charges were filed against anybody. They had a suspect . . . they even informed him of his rights . . . but they didn't feel confident enough they had the evidence to convict the man."

Feldman continued with the good and the bad aspects of Sam Hugh's life. Sam Hugh liked to drink, and if he hadn't had too many, he was a good conversationalist. He was sharp and witty and had a knack for understanding human conditions. Nobody could fool him. He hated people with pretentions, and when he'd talk about them, you just had to laugh and say to yourself, "Sam Hugh's plenty smart, all right."

"Sam Hugh was the kind of lawyer often found in Southern literature. Every small town has the brilliant legal minds who don't want to live up to the expectations the world has set for them. People are shocked by their rejection of small town values, but what's remarkable about these non-conformists is that they insist on staying in their home towns. 'This is what I am,' they seem to be saying, 'and what are you going to do about it?'"

Feldman closed his editorial with these words: "Sam Hugh Park—attorney, antique collector, son of the family that published *The Press Argus* for almost half a century—did not have an easy time in this world, and perhaps he will now find the peace that eluded him here."

CHAPTER NINETEEN

Sheriff Ball attended Sam Hugh Park's funeral. Even though most of the lawmen believed a guilty man was buried that day, the sheriff had his doubts. He had nothing but a hunch to go on, but most of the time, his hunches turned out to be correct. He thought Sam Hugh was too gentle a man to kill his mother, and he had acted genuine in his grief when he discovered her dead body. He didn't know who killed Ruie Ann Park, but he'd prayed for two years that he would solve this murder, and he was a man who believed in prayer.

He did not, however, believe that anyone, besides Jesus, could rise from the dead.

The Alamos believed they were a gift from God and thus Christlike. The previous April of 1982 when Linda Alamo died of cancer, her husband, Tony, insisted that her body lay on display at their home while the followers prayed for her resurrection. This was utter stupidity, Sheriff Ball thought, and he began distancing himself from the compound in Dyer. Tony and his followers were already in trouble with the Feds for claiming their businesses were religious in nature and therefore tax exempt. And anyway, how could a body rise if it had been embalmed? Or had it? Whatever the case, Susan Alamo was eventually entombed in a concrete memorial that sat on the property.

The sheriff's wife consoled her husband during the hard days—the days when he was chastised for not solving the murder, for not nailing Sam Hugh Park's hide to the gallows, for being too dumb, and the worst criticism of all, that he should go back to working at Snoddy-Pratt's, a hardware store in Alma.

Mr. Snoddy was a successful businessman who loved politics, and he had made an unsuccessful run for governor. The sheriff wished he could talk to Mr. Snoddy, but he'd died in 1975. His son-in-law, Zeke Pratt, and Mr. Snoddy's daughter, Mary, ran the store now. Neither one of them expressed their opinions one way or the other. Mary said the whole thing was a tragedy, and no family should ever suffer like the Park family had. Trellon thought that just about summed it up. It wasn't only a murder case, but a case that centered on a family with a whole lot of secrets.

CHAPTER TWENTY

After Sam Hugh's funeral, only a few friends gathered around the kitchen table at the Winter Palace. Linda Myers had brought over a tray of chocolate chip cookies and a pecan pie. Sam Hugh's sister, Linda, ate a cookie and asked for coffee, which prompted Linda Myers to get the coffee pot going.

But before the coffee finished perking, Howard had announced that it was time to leave.

"Why?" Linda asked. "I'd like to visit a little more and have my coffee."

"The weather's bad, and I want to get home."

"Okay then, but let me gather my things I've left in the bathroom."

"Make it quick. I'll go warm up the car."

Linda and Howard drove home to Cabot in silence. She stared out the window, deep in memories of the first time she saw her brother. At age seven, she was taller than he and a year older. She was happy about it because, as she realized quickly, that was the only achievement she would ever have over the magnificent Sam Hugh Park.

Sam Hugh was not a full-term baby when he entered the world. Frightened that something would happen to him and he would die like her first-born, a little girl who only lived a few days, his mother kept him inside and away from outside germs. As he grew older, she dressed him up in cute little outfits to show him off at school, church, and music recitals. She was positive his intellect was far above the other boys his age. Believing he was a child prodigy, his mother enrolled him in music lessons taught by Mrs. Harry David Bryan, who, she believed, was the only teacher in town who could develop Sam Hugh's musical aptitude. He was smothered by his mother, and those who knew both Sam Hugh and his mother spoke of their concerns to each other. They believed it was Ruie Ann's fault that her son was homosexual.

Linda was told she was on loan from the orphanage because her biological mother wouldn't sign the adoption papers. She felt like she officially belonged nowhere, and then, years later, when she finally was officially adopted, she still had the same lost feeling.

At first she liked it with the Park family. There was plenty to eat, and her new mother bought her pretty clothes to wear, but soon she realized it was all for show. Her mother liked to show off the little girl she had picked out at the orphanage. She thought that would make the other mothers in Van Buren think highly of her altruistic spirit. It didn't work. Her mother went to various club meetings, some of which she was a founding member, but she was not well-liked, and none of the women asked her over for coffee or to meet them for lunch—except for Mrs. Scroggins, who was interested in genealogy, as was Ruie Ann, who traced her relatives back to the Mayflower.

"Those aren't *your* relatives, Linda," her mother told her. "They're your brother's."

As if Linda really cared.

"To hell with the Mayflower," she said under her breath every time her mother mentioned it.

She liked her daddy better. He seemed more relaxed, and she lovingly recalled the time, just weeks after she came to live with them, that she and her new daddy walked to town in the February snow. She was happy, and the pictures of her in a snowsuit with her mother's writing that read *Linda walks to town with Dady in the snow February 1948* in the photo album proved it. She smiled, remembering how her mother always misspelled the word "daddy."

Howard broke the silence by asking, "You didn't take anything from the house, did you? I'm going to come back and get Sam Hugh's office furniture, but that's all. You hear me? That is all."

Linda would have liked to take the family album but didn't. She did sneak her father's pipes and four plates out by packing them in her overnight case.

Ice was forming on the trees that lined I-40 as they slowly passed the exits for Mulberry, Ozark, Clarksville, and Russellville. The sand trucks had been out, making the interstate passable.

"Things are going to change at home," Howard said. "No more moping about and staying up half the night. You are going to sleep when I go to sleep and get up when I get up."

Linda wished they would hit a slick spot and career off the road, upside down into a ditch full of icy water. She wished that Howard would drown, and she would miraculously survive with only a runner in her hose. She would rush home to her three boys and tell them that Daddy had gone to heaven, and they wouldn't even cry. Oh, she wished that would happen. And she wished his girlfriend would die in the car with him.

She could feel her eyes sting and fill with tears. She'd had a hard time controlling her emotions since her mother's death. She couldn't sleep, so she went to her family doctor, begging him to promise that he wouldn't tell Howard he had prescribed Ambien for her. That helped for a while, but she had to stop when she realized she was, once again, pregnant. The child had not been conceived in love but in fear that if she didn't submit to Howard's urges he would surely leave her for Judy. How could she make it alone without a paycheck and four boys to feed and clothe and educate? How could she make it another day with Howard lording over her?

CHAPTER TWENTY-ONE

Linda knew her marriage was over. She also knew with all her heart that she didn't want a divorce. Trying harder than ever to please the father of her children, she finally realized nothing was going to fix her marriage.

Howard moved out of the home they had worked and saved for since their marriage in 1965. He moved in with his mother, which he said was preferable to living with a skinny, crazy woman.

Linda was desperately sad that summer and fall of 1983, so she agreed to file for divorce. Howard gave her the name of a lawyer in Jacksonville, and she hired him to represent her. The divorce was final two days before Christmas. She had agreed to move after Christmas was over and let Howard keep the house. Howard had convinced her it was more important for the older boys to get to stay in the home they'd lived in all their lives.

"I basically walked away with nothing," Linda confided to Guila Turner, a friend from the days when she taught school in North Little Rock. They had lived close to each other, and even though Guila was twenty years older, she offered Linda unconditional friendship.

Guila had known Howard since he was a boy growing up in North Little Rock and had never liked him. Or his mother.

Guila poured another cup of coffee for Linda as they sat in Guila's kitchen in Lakeview, a middle-class neighborhood in North Little Rock. Guila's kitchen was warm and smelled sweetly of the apple bread she had just taken out of the oven.

"After all you did for him, the shit-ass."

Linda smiled as she stirred a teaspoon of sugar into her coffee.

"Oh, Guila, the things that come out of your mouth."

Guila was a beautiful woman. She was tall and thin and always wore good-looking clothes. Cuss words coming from a classy lady like Guila just didn't add up.

"Well, you put him through law school, which he barely finished because he was not the smartest apple on the tree. And then when he failed the bar examination the first time, he blamed it on you. Got you pregnant with four little boys, and now he says you can keep the ones who need their diapers changed, and he'll take the older ones."

"I have to get a job, Guila. I need a paycheck coming in every month. After Mom died, Sam Hugh spent all the money from her. The sale of the house only netted about fifty thousand. I've got to save that for the kids. Howard says he'll invest that for me."

"Don't you dare let him get his hands on that money! Those boys will never see a cent of it."

Linda looked out the window into the rainy April morning. The glass was fogged from the heat in the kitchen, and it reminded her of her own mind.

"I've been in a fog since my mother died."

"Well, don't think about that now. You've got to deal with the present, and that is what's most important."

Sam Hugh's old car was all she had to drive. The tires on her yellow VW bug wobbled, and she'd been told by a mechanic that it wasn't safe to drive. Howard had told her that was nonsense, and the mechanic just wanted to get his money. Howard was always afraid people were out to cheat him. Linda remembered a restaurant meal he had refused to pay for, and once he'd refused to pay a contractor he'd hired to make several home repairs. She had been embarrassed many times by his bullying behavior, even demanding refunds from a movie he didn't like because he felt it was pro-Communist.

"I'm going to speak frank with you," Guila said, as if she had never spoken frankly before. "You've tried a geographic solution by moving first to Fort Smith and then back to North Little Rock. You belong in Cabot, where your kids are and where they belong. You have friends there. Ask them for help. Nobody of any importance likes Howard. And I hear he's bought a ten thousand dollar diamond engagement ring for his whore."

"What? He doesn't have money like that to spend on a ring."

"That's what I heard," Guila said. "And on good authority."

Linda felt like she would faint. Only she knew how deeply depressed she was over the divorce. She tried to hide her unhappiness, just like she had to do all her life—in the orphanage, at her home in Van Buren, and with her husband who had promised to love and protect her.

"Oh, Guila, who told you that?"

"Your friends in Cabot. I had about four phone calls in one day."

"Well, that money must be what the boys inherited from Howard's granny's timber land. Howard said he was going to invest that money for their college education. Oh, that man!"

"You have got to stand up for yourself. Take him back to court and get a fair settlement this time. He railroaded you, and you let him. Get some backbone, girl."

Linda felt tears sliding down her cheeks. Her shoulders shook, and the tears became sobs, loud wracking sobs she was powerless to stop. It seemed like she would never stop crying. Thank goodness she was with Guila. Dear, sweet Guila, who could cuss as well as any sailor.

By the time Linda left to pick up her babies from the sitter's, the sky was a swath of purple and mauve and yellow. She was exhausted, but she also felt a little better. With Guila's help and guidance and the friendship of her Cabot pals, she vowed to stand up to Howard, even if it meant going back to court.

She sat down at the kitchen table with pad and pencil and wrote down exactly what she would ask him for. (1) She wanted her house back. (2) She wanted alimony and child support. (3) She wanted a decent car with the title under her name alone. (4) She wanted her boys to live together under one roof—hers.

CHAPTER TWENTY-TWO

Linda moved back to Cabot and rented a little house at 47 Robinson Street, barely large enough for her and the two younger boys. The older ones, as the divorce decree stated, would continue to live with their father. But she was going to change that.

Linda made plans to seek employment, find a babysitter for the boys, and try to start life all over again. She was still plagued by despair and felt like she was barely able to dress herself and the boys. But she had to do it. Her babies needed her.

She worried about the older boys being with their father. When they visited her, they told her they didn't like being at their house without her, and that sometimes they didn't get to eat supper because their dad was never home.

She knew where he was of course. With Judy.

The madder she got about Judy and the engagement ring, the madder she got at Howard. She began to wonder if either of them were capable of raising four boys. She remembered her days in the orphanage, and she knew that nobody wanted to adopt older boys. She began plotting a way to try to have the boys tested to see if they were progressing like they should in school. She knew they both needed prodding to make good grades, and if Howard wasn't around to make them do their homework, they would fail in school. She couldn't let that happen.

The only positive thing about living in the small rental house was that she started sleeping better. No longer did she have to take two sleeping pills—one was enough. And there was no one to tell her when to go to sleep or what TV shows to watch. The boys dictated her schedule now, and she didn't have to obey Howard another minute. As the days went by, she gained a little confidence, but there was never enough money. And she heard that the older boys were not taken care of properly. No breakfast, an apple for lunch, and supper was usually a hamburger from Hardee's.

But the news that Howard and Judy were going to have a big, fancy wedding in the Baptist Church shocked her. How stupid was that? This would be Judy's third marriage, and everybody knew how strict the Baptists were about divorcees marrying in the church. At least, in the Cabot Baptist Church.

Somehow the news of their pending marriage gave Linda a little spark. Enough of a spark to set her mind to formulate a plan that would help take Howard back to court. The spark escalated to a fire when she received a phone call from Judy's former husband inquiring about the possibility of him and Linda pursuing an alienation of affection suit against Judy and Howard.

Linda called Guila.

"Should I do it?"

Guila, happy to hear some spunk in Linda's voice, said, "Sue the bastard. He's beat you down until you can barely leave your house. You have a lot of people in Cabot on your side, what with your teaching and library connections. Go for it, and I'll be in your corner every step of the way. So will your preacher and the deacons and the members of the choir and the Sunday School teachers and the piano player and the organist and even the goddamn janitor."

Linda laughed, and Guila believed that was the first time she'd heard her friend laugh in a long, long time. She vowed to take Linda out to lunch once a week. She'd take her shopping and maybe convince her to get a different hairdo. Guila had good taste in clothes, and her motto was quality over quantity. Unlike Linda, she had never worn a dress from Wal-Mart.

Linda prayed every night. Most often, she knelt at the side of her bed. She thanked God for giving her a friend like Guila. She asked God to keep her boys safe. And she asked for forgiveness for her sins.

CHAPTER TWENTY-THREE

Linda felt comfort in the number of phone calls she received from her Cabot friends. Friends she played bridge with and friends she taught with had not abandoned her.

"It's not right, what he did to you, Linda," a dentist's wife told her. "Nobody liked Howard. They just put up with him because of you."

Soon, she was scouring the want ads, and after finding several that looked promising, she circled them in red pencil. One was for a "Girl Friday" at an insurance firm, and another was for a salesperson at Dillard's at Park Plaza in Little Rock.

Around noon on June thirteenth, Howard called her and asked her to come to his office. His voice was friendly enough.

"Do you mind coming down to my office tomorrow? There are some things I'd like to talk to you about."

Linda couldn't control her shaky voice.

"Uh, what about?"

"Oh, nothing for either of us to worry about. I just thought we needed to nail down some of our visitation rules that, frankly, neither one of us has been following."

"Okay. I could come tomorrow afternoon. Say three o'clock?"

"Make it four."

She thought about arguing, but she had made a vow to Guila to choose her battles.

"Okay."

The next day, Linda dressed in her green outfit, the one she had worn on an interview that had seemed promising. The human resource director had said he'd call her back real soon.

As she was leaving, a friend from Bible study called.

"I've been thinking, Linda. I've been thinking that I should go with you to Howard's office. He might have some trick up his sleeve."

Linda laughed. "That's silly, Martha. You're the second person who has called me today. What do you all think he's going to do? Kill me?

She told her babysitter she'd be back in two hours. The high school senior charged three dollars an hour for both the little boys. She'd be with Howard no more than an hour, she was sure, and then she would have time to go to Safeway. She kissed the boys, who were watching *Sesame Street*, and drove to Howard's office.

CHAPTER TWENTY-FOUR

When Linda returned with two sacks of groceries from Safeway, she set them down on the dinette table. Her visit with Howard had been emotionally draining, and she had cried all the way home, and even while standing in the produce aisle at the grocery store. Howard had told her he received the letter from her attorney threatening him with an alienation of affection suit, and he'd said a lot of mean things to her. They fought about the number of visits each had with one child or the other, and even though Linda promised herself that she wouldn't mention Judy Harper's name, she did.

She paid the sitter, changed into jeans and a blue-and-white striped shirt, and took the boys outside to play in their sandbox. She wondered when she would ever have some peace of mind.

Around six, Howard telephoned, acting as nice as could be.

"Linda, I'd like to take all the boys to the movies. I think they would enjoy that. We'll go to Wendy's first and then on to North Little Rock for the movie. *E.T.* is playing at the cheap movies. I hear that's a good, decent movie."

Shocked by the invitation because he'd never taken all four boys anywhere at the same time before, she agreed to have them ready by six.

"Boys," she called through the kitchen screen door, "come inside and get your bath. Your daddy is going to take you to the movies. Won't that be something?"

Later, when Howard knocked on the front door, she had Johnny and Bobby dressed in their best outfits, hair parted, and shirts tucked in. She walked them to the door and expected to see the older boys waiting in the car.

"Where are Carl and Harry? Aren't they going?"

"Oh, sure. I'm going back to pick them up. You know those guys. They're never on time."

Linda handed Howard a paper sack with two extra diapers, in case Johnny had an accident. She kissed each one, waved goodbye, and went into the kitchen to put up the groceries. She'd forgotten about the popsicles, and they had melted into a puddle at the bottom of the sack. She had too much on her mind, she told herself, and began to cry.

Around seven thirty, she answered a loud knock on the front door. She opened it and recognized Wayne Hicks and another man, who was introduced to her as Van Buren's Chief of Police, Gary Robertson. The men standing behind them wore Cabot police uniforms.

"Linda," Robertson said, "may we come in? There's something very important we need to talk to you about."

What in the world, she thought. *What's going on?* But she smiled and pushed open the screen door.

"Is there a table we could sit at?" Hicks asked.

Linda led them into her kitchen and motioned to the small table by the window.

"What's this about?" she asked.

"We have some new information about your mom's murder," Robertson said.

Linda's face lost its rosy color and faded to a pale gray.

"Oh? What is it?"

Robertson cleared his throat. "We've got a warrant for your arrest for the murder of your mother, Ruie Ann Park." He pulled out a white sheet of paper from his inside coat pocket. "We have this bench warrant that charges you with murder in the first degree, a class Y felony."

With her lips moving, she read the document, and Hicks thought at first he saw some relief in her face. But then she gasped and put her hand to her mouth.

She listened as Hicks read her rights, and she held herself together long enough to sign a piece of paper he placed in front of her. She felt like her heart would stop beating any minute. Her voice was a whisper, and the words she wanted to say wouldn't come out.

"We need you to come to Van Buren with us." Hicks spoke louder, as if he thought she hadn't heard him.

Linda tried to stand up, but she didn't know if her legs would support her.

"What?"

"We have evidence to support this arrest."

"But my children? What about my babies?"

Gary Robertson placed his hand on her shoulder.

"Your husband will take care of them. We made arrangements for him to keep the children. The younger ones, I mean. He already has the older boys, right?"

Poor girl, he thought. There is no way she could have done such a thing. She was so little, so shy. But yet he had heard the tapes.

"How long will I be gone? Should I pack an overnight bag?" Linda said. She was in the middle of a heavy period. She'd need to take some Kotex and maybe a change of underwear.

"No, you have to come right now."

"My purse. Can I take my purse?"

Wayne Hicks looked to the police chief, who nodded his head yes.

"Okay, grab your purse."

109

She walked into her bedroom and retrieved the purse that she habitually kept on the door handle. Her hands were shaking so wildly that she had trouble holding on to it.

"Dear God," she wailed, holding on to the bed for support. "How did they find out? Who told the police?"

Hicks stood in the hall, leaning against the wall. He held his head down and rubbed his right shoe against the cheap beige carpet that had been stained by previous renters.

"You need to use the rest room?" he asked Linda.

She told him she didn't, but she would like to get a glass of water. Her mouth was dry, and she felt like she might be sick.

"Go ahead," Hicks said. "Can I have one, too, please?"

Chief Robertson rotated his shoulders and sighed, and Hicks knew he was getting angry at the delay.

"Don't be long," Hicks said, following Linda into the kitchen

Robertson was anxious to get back to Van Buren at a reasonable hour. It had been a long, hard day. He looked at his watch. He'd been up since five, driven to Little Rock, and conferred with the state police investigator before they drove to Cabot. He'd had nothing but coffee all day, and he realized he needed something in his stomach or his ulcer would give him trouble.

"We'll stop on the road and get something to go," Robertson said.

Linda handed a small plastic glass to Hicks.

"You can tell I've got little kids, can't you?"

He held the little Mickey Mouse cup in his hand.

"This will be just fine."

Robertson looked at his watch again and opened the front door.

"Mrs. Martin, I have to handcuff you. Please put your arms in front of you."

Linda did as she was told. She'd seen on *Law and Order* that handcuffs were supposed to hurt. These only felt heavy, and she was relieved they didn't seem tight.

"Let's go," Robertson said. He helped her down the sidewalk and opened the police car's rear door and motioned for Linda to get in.

Hicks sat in the driver's seat, turned the key, and slid the gearshift into drive. He paused, looked both ways.

"Uh, I can't remember whether to turn right or left."

Linda leaned forward and tapped him on the shoulder.

"Turn right."

Hicks drove very fast, Linda thought. She could see the dashboard from where she sat, and the gauge was steady at eighty miles an hour. He also had the air conditioner blasting cold air, and when she touched her nose, she wasn't surprised to find it cold. Should she ask him to turn it down?

The other guy, the police chief, was leaning against the window of the passenger side. He was impressed, she thought, with his title. He wore shiny cowboy boots, and on his red tie was a tie clasp that depicted a pair of handcuffs.

Even though Hicks was obese, he seemed nicer and more polite. He had gone to high school with her, but Robertson must have been from somewhere else.

Out the window, she saw the lights of Conway, and the traffic was heavy with a steady stream of trucks. She had already counted three Wal-Mart trucks. This was a highway she had traveled many times. She couldn't remember a time when she had driven it while in a happy mood. Every time she had gone home to Van Buren, her mother had demanded it, and her husband was mad that she had gone. She couldn't win with them. Ruie hated Howard. Howard hated Ruie. She felt tears on her cheeks, and she blotted them with her arm. What was going to happen when they got to Van Buren? She cried harder, but this time she let the tears fall, not caring enough about herself to conceal them. It seemed to Linda that she had been crying all her life.

CHAPTER TWENTY-FIVE

Hicks, Robertson, and—as Robertson referred to Linda on the radio—"the female Caucasian prisoner," left Cabot around eight o'clock at night, headed for Van Buren, on Thursday, June fourteenth, 1984. It had been a month over three years since Ruie Ann Park had been found murdered in her home. Hicks kept watching Linda in his rearview mirror. She was crying quietly, and he occasionally heard her moan like someone coming out of surgery.

They had stopped at a McDonald's in Morrilton to get something to go, but Linda refused so much as a Coke. The assistant chief ordered a chocolate milkshake and fries, thinking those items would be easy to eat and drink while he was driving.

Linda was curled up on the seat with her back resting against the door. She looked out the window, and when Hicks tried talking to her, she wouldn't reply.

He and the chief decided to play the tape for Linda about the time they got to Ozark. Hicks didn't think it was the best idea, but Robertson insisted.

"Let her know what we got," he said. "She'll be putty in our hands by the time we pull into the police parking lot. I've already notified the office to have the newspapers and television folks there."

Hicks didn't like the idea. It seemed unnecessarily cruel to let Linda hear that her ex-husband had turned her in for murdering her mom. Howard Martin had called the police chief on Wednesday and told him that he knew who killed Ruie Ann Park. If they could arrange to have his office wired, he'd lure his ex-wife down there and get her to confess so they could get it on tape. Hicks surmised Howard Martin had made a deal, so no charges would ever be brought against him concerning his prior knowledge in the case.

Hicks kept going over in his mind the events of the last couple of days. Suddenly, after three years of being absolutely certain that Sam Hugh Park had killed his mother, Hicks found out that he probably didn't. The poor queer guy had gone to his grave knowing that everybody in the whole state of Arkansas, and most of Oklahoma, was certain he killed his mother.

What kind of man would turn in his own wife? An ex-wife, but still—she was the mother of his four children. Hicks thought of his dear wife, Wanda. He'd stand beside her no matter what she did. He guessed Howard Martin wanted to get Linda out of his life. With her in prison, he'd have all the boys under his wing, including any inheritance that came their way. When Mrs. Park died, she'd left the bulk of her estate to Sam Hugh. She left Linda one of the rent houses. And then when Sam Hugh Park died, everything that Sam Hugh hadn't spent went to Linda, and if she was found guilty of killing her mother, then what?

He felt horribly embarrassed that he and the sheriff and the state police had rushed to judgment in thinking that just because a guy was a queer and a drunk he'd automatically be the one-and-only suspect in his mom's murder. He had asked Linda Martin where she was at the time of the death of her mother, and she had told them she was home in Cabot, three hours away. They'd accepted what she said, and that was it. But now, as he thought back on the crime scene, he remembered that long, black hairs were clutched in the dead woman's hand. Sam Hugh didn't have black hair, but his sister did. *Oh my God*, Hicks thought. *We were so sure Sam Hugh did it.*

CHAPTER TWENTY-SIX

Hicks saw the exits for Ozark, and following instructions from the police chief, he inserted a cassette into the player. He didn't turn it on until he warned Linda.

"I'm fixing to play a tape that was made this afternoon in your husband's office," he said, watching for her reaction in the rear-view mirror.

He saw her turn her eyes from the window, and she sat up straight, locking eyes with him in the mirror. "You taped my meeting with Howard today?"

"Yes, ma'am. It was his idea."

And then he pushed the play button.

> Howard: Okay, send her in. How you doing? Well, you look awfully nice.
>
> Linda: Thanks. Well, I went to a job interview.
>
> Howard: Well, how did it go?
>
> Linda: Uh, great. I think pretty good. I don't know. It was . . .

Howard: Who'd you interview with?

Linda: Uh, New York Mutual Insurance. Excellent job.

Howard: Secretarial job, or what?

Linda: Yeah, it's a Girl Friday for the head
of management.

Howard: Well, that's great.

Linda: Eleven thousand, it pays.

Howard: Well, good.

Linda: And I know they liked me—she, the girl who
interviewed me, and the man. He was really nice.

Howard: Good.

Linda: Now the one yesterday paid eight hundred and
twenty-five dollars, and those are the only two good
jobs I've really been to. The others have been—

Howard: Well, you looked awfully nice going in there.

Linda: I wanted to wear something like this, so I wore
my blue outfit yesterday.

Howard: Well, it's best not to wear green, I mean, not
to wear red.

Linda: Yeah.

Howard: When you interview.

Linda: Yeah, well, I haven't. I wore the blue one, and I
wore the green one today but so I have to keep straight
which one—'cause both of them, if they like me, they
will call me back.

Howard: Now you know this weekend, I want to pick the kids up.

Linda: This weekend?

Howard: Yeah, isn't this Father's Day weekend?

Linda: Well, you didn't let me have them last week.

Howard: Well, you had them two weeks in a row at Mother's Day.

Linda: Okay, well, I haven't had them in . . . I guess you can go ahead. I thought—

Howard: Are you trying to say I'm visiting with my kids too much?

Linda: No, you just said I was going to have them last weekend, and I didn't get them. You remember? I said why don't we change so—

Howard: Well, yeah, but when I decided to go swimming—

Linda: Oh, well—

Howard: You said you didn't have to have them.

Linda: Well, it's been about three—

Howard: Have I had them three weeks in a row?

Linda: Let's see. Last weekend . . . well, it would have been if . . . you did let me keep them one Saturday. You said I couldn't, but then you relented and let them come Friday night and then Saturday night. I guess I—

Howard: Well, I'd like to be with all four of them on Father's Day.

Linda: Well, that's what I was thinking. Well—

Howard: 'Cause you sure were on Mother's Day. Well, what do you know?

Linda: Uh . . . oh, did you get my letter from Mr. Clark?

Howard: No, why?

Linda: Well, you're supposed to get one.

Secretary's voice: Here's some stuff that came in today. I just haven't had the chance to bring it to you.

Howard: All right.

Secretary's voice: All right.

Howard: Why don't you shut that door. Change of custody? Of all four children? (now reading from the letter) "We want an accounting from you as to the value of the marital residence, the rental house owned by the pension plan or profit sharing plan, the value of your interest in Thompson, O'Brien, and Martin"—they misspelled O'Brien. They need an accounting of the actual value of the stock of drive computer. Well, it's not Drive Computer, it's Prime Computer. An accounting as to the value of gold and silver, the value of the jointly owned furniture and household goods, the value of '75 VW Rabbit, the '76 Chevrolet Station wagon, the 1980 Chevette. "You should account to Mrs. Martin for the use of the twelve thousand five hundred dollars borrowed prior to the divorce and for the amount of anything received by you and placed in a joint checking account."

Howard: Well, that's what you bought the stock with what you got . . . I didn't want anything . . . you got the stock. We borrowed the money from Mother.

Howard: (Reading from the letter again) "In addition, it has come to our attention that you are living with a woman to whom you are not wed, and we object to the children being subjected to your present living situation. You should also be advised that Mrs. Martin has authorized me to file an alienation of affection suit against Judy Harper."

(Howard stops reading.)

Howard: Well, of course, you know there's no bargaining because I'm not going to give up the children at all—

Linda: Well, uh, the children . . . The bargaining will be done by the courts on the children. It has come to my attention that they are abused and neglected mentally, cruelly. I will not make the decision on the children. They are going to be tested psychologically. They . . . I think that should be up to the counselor who works with them and the judge, the lawyers, or whoever if . . . Those children are in a bad way, Howard. Not just me. And I've got . . . I've got plenty of evidence that I would rather them go to a foster home and be cared for. You just don't realize what you've done to them.

Howard: Well, let me ask you this—

Linda: If not with me, then someone else.

Howard: Don't you think it's just a little bit hypocritical for you to kill your mother and then accuse me of the things that you've accused me of?

Linda: *No.* (whispering)

Howard: You don't think it's hypocritical?

Linda: *No.* (whispering)

Howard: You don't see any inconsistencies?

Linda: Howard, I didn't mean to do what I did.

Howard: But you did it.

Linda: But yours was a plain execution, what you did. You knew—I had tried to bargain with you the whole time—you knew when you made up that divorce what you did. I didn't know.

Howard: I don't think what I'm being blamed of is nearly as bad as what you've done.

Linda: Howard, can you . . . ? I did something terrible, and I know it. But you have done—

Howard: Let me ask you one thing—

Linda: You have broken some yourself. You've broken at least three of them.

Howard: Three what?

Linda: You have broken three of the Ten Commandments.

Howard: What have I broken?

Linda: I think you've committed adultery.

Howard: No, I did not.

Linda: There isn't anybody I—

Howard: I didn't sleep with any other women as long as we were married.

Linda: Howard, I know you've lied and you've cheated and you stole. You know good and well—

Howard: Be specific, Linda. Where did I lie?

Linda: You lied to me.

Howard: About what?

Linda: That divorce. You . . . you knew you were stealing when you put down all that stuff. You lied when you fixed the papers.

Howard: Let me tell you . . . I told you all I wanted was the home and I . . . listen to me, now—

Linda: You're lying right there. You did not.

Howard: Will you . . . ? You better listen to me. I told you all I wanted was the home and for you to—you could have everything else—make a list of what you wanted. And you did it, and that's exactly what you got.

Linda: Howard, that's right. I got nothing, hardly.

Howard: You made the list.

Linda: You put my inheritance in there.

Howard: Let's . . . let's talk about that—

Linda: (Yelling) I wasn't in any condition to make any list!

Howard: Keep your voice down. Keep your voice down. Shh, keep it down.

Linda: (Still yelling) I didn't even know that you had cheated on me until I came back in April, and then it was later on that I realized!

Howard: Keep your voice down. I don't want anybody in this office to know what we're talking about. To begin with, Linda, any woman that murders her own mother is not entitled to an inheritance. Our children ought to have what you got.

Linda: They will have it.

Howard: When?

Linda: It's going to be in trusts for them, and it is for them. It certainly will go to them. It's going to be tied up so tight that nobody will ever be able to touch a penny until they come of age.

Howard: But you're going to run through it before they get it.

Linda: I am not—

Howard: But you're not entitled to it for one second

Linda: I am not going to use it. I have had nothing to use except that. How'd you think . . . ?

Howard: You don't understand. You weren't entitled to your mother's estate. Listen to me—

Linda: I know that.

Howard: For one second.

Linda: I know that.

Howard: And there's nothing in here in this property settlement. You got your mother's estate. You got Sam Hugh's estate.

Linda: I didn't get anything from Sam Hugh's yet. Maybe down the road I will. I have not gotten one penny, and I won't.

Howard: Hold on . . . but you got it. Had I known that you were going to give me the problems that you are giving me, I might . . . if I'd been able to look into that crystal ball, I might have done something about it to ensure that you wouldn't get a dadgum thing.

Linda: Well, I can take it, and I can put it up for them. I haven't got it to put up for them. I am not asking, Howard. I have tried to bargain with you this whole time of the divorce, when I realized what you had done to me. I never tried to take advantage of you in the divorce.

Howard: Let me tell you something—

Linda: I know—

Howard: I want to tell you the way I feel.

Linda: I know the way you feel.

Howard: How do I feel?

Linda: And I know about how you feel about those children.

Howard: Well, how do I feel?

Linda: You don't give a damn. That's exactly how you feel.

Howard: I certainly do.

Linda: You do not. If you loved those children, you wouldn't treat them . . . and you wouldn't allow that woman to treat them like that.

Howard: Let me tell you something, Linda. The only reason I stayed in that marriage to you was because of the children.

Linda: I'm not talking about that now.

Howard: You know good and well—

Linda: (Shouting) So that entitles you—

Howard: Shh, keep your voice down.

Linda: I am not screaming. So that entitles you to just take everything and deprive your children of what belongs to them?

Howard: I love my children, Linda.

Linda: No, you don't. Don't say that. I know you don't.

Howard: Do you remember the night you told me you killed your mother. I stayed in the marriage only because of our children.

Linda: Well, I'm trying to help them now.

Howard: Well, what are you trying to do for them?

Linda: Listen, with that inheritance . . . it will be put up for them.

Howard: Are you trying to tell me that the children will be better off with a—

Linda: No.

Howard: Listen to me. A murderess than with their own father?

Linda: I care about them. I do more for them than you do. I know what kind of life they're having right now. I've had other people tell me. I know exactly what they're going to have. Just like they're having now. Oh, they're having lots of fun, aren't they? You couldn't care less about them. I've heard stories about them being alone, by themselves.

Howard: When?

Linda: I have somebody who will sign a statement. Nine thirty at night, she came home.

Howard: Oh, you're crazy.

Linda: I am not crazy. I know good and well what's happening to those children.

Howard: There's no way—

Linda: You don't care about them.

Howard: The boys have never been left alone.

Linda: My friend says she went to your door and nobody was home, and Carl was down the street, sitting on the corner.

Howard: Let me tell you, if I ran to the grocery store, maybe, but I never left those children alone. You can get all your witnesses together, and we'll just take it out in court.

Linda: Well, we will. I don't care where the children go, but I want them cared for, and they're not being cared for. You know they're not.

Howard: Do you care for them as much as you cared for your mother?

Linda: No, I love the children more. I'd do anything for them.

Howard: Do you love them more than you loved your brother?

Linda: Yes, yes I do.

Howard: Because Sam Hugh would be alive today if it wasn't for you. If you'd gone to Van Buren the way I told you to, he might be alive today.

Linda: Howard, all I want for these children is to . . . I want to give them a home, and I want to do the best for them. If the courts say, "Hey, they're perfectly fine." But you're not doing a thing for them. I know what you're doing. I've had too many people tell me.

Howard: Well, if you're going to believe the gossip that I'm sure you're stirring up.

Linda: Howard, listen. They don't have to live with me. All I want is for them to live with someone who'll take care of them and love them and not just . . . Well, you know how you're doing.

Howard: So you're serious about wanting the children? This letter says you want the children. Are you serious?

Linda: You know I want them, but I know you don't want me to have them, so what I'll do is I'll do whatever the court says—if the court says. I want them tested. I want some testing done on Carl. He's not doing well, and we don't know about the others.

Howard: Listen, you talk about the psychology of the children. Well, I want to know one thing. You know you told me that you left little Bobby in the car the night you went to your mother's? And you told me he stayed in the car. That he did not go in the house. Is that correct?

Linda: Yes.

Howard: You're not saying that very convincingly.

Linda: Yes, I am.

Howard: Then what was the mattress doing in there between your mother's room and the kitchen?

Linda: I don't know, but it wasn't for Bobby. He stayed in the car. He was asleep.

Howard: So you and your mother just had a nice long discussion while the child sat outside.

Linda: He was asleep.

Howard: Your mother didn't want to see him?

Linda: I just told you. He did not go into the house.

Howard: You promise me?

Linda: Yes, Howard . . . I just . . . Yes, Howard.

Howard: You know, you talk about psychological trauma to a child. If he saw you kill your mother, he'd never get over that.

Linda: No, he did not. He was in the car. Howard—

Howard: How do I know? How do I know you're telling the truth about Bobby being in the car?

Linda: You'll just have to take my word. But he was in the car. I do know that. If the . . . what I feel like . . . if the children . . . I'm not happy with the situation with the children, and you know that. I think you've done something. You've done a lot of foolish things in the last couple of months, and if the counselor...I want them tested.

Howard: When you get a court order, then they'll get a testing, but not otherwise.

Linda: I want them tested. You know they need it.

Howard: You get a court order, and then they'll be tested but—

Linda: I want them tested, and I want them . . . I—

Howard: You're trying to ruin me, aren't you?

Linda: No. I'm not. I'm not trying to ruin you. Howard, you know that I worked in that marriage, and I'm entitled to part of it. You told me I wasn't entitled to anything. My lawyer says I'm entitled to half of everything, across the board.

Howard: Linda—

Linda: I have . . . when I came to you before—

Howard: I told you that you weren't entitled to the pension plan.

Linda: I know that. That house isn't a pension plan.

Howard: That's right.

Linda: He says right across the board, I'm entitled to half.

Howard: I know that's right.

Linda: I have tried to work. I never came in and . . . and said I want this, and I want this, and I want this. I asked for a fair distribution. That's all I ask.

Howard: Honey, I told you to sit down and write up a list, and you could have everything you wanted, except I wanted the house.

Linda: No . . . you . . . never said that.

Howard: There's your lie.

Linda: I said, Howard . . . you told me, oh, I'm gonna date and all. You told me, if you'll remember, you told me flat out. You know you demolished me.

Howard: Let me tell you—

Linda: No—

Howard: I just want to say something—

Linda: You know I wanted that home because that's where all my children had been. They were raised there, but I can live in another home. It's the children. I know how they feel. Howard, now before I had nothing. Nothing that I could use as a wedge. You know that. There was nothing—

Howard: You know—

Linda: I'm trying to work out a settlement.

Howard: Let me ask you this—

Linda: And I want to tell you, those are ugly things that I have against you, and you have something ugly against me. All the things we've got against each other would totally destroy your career and my life. And the four children would be in limbo. Three of them would go to homes, and one would be in a juvenile delinquent home, probably. Because nobody wants a fourteen-year-old.

Howard: Well—

Linda: And that's exactly what it—

Howard: You've got me kind of over a barrel because you know that I do love the children enough that—

Linda: If you loved them, why did you treat them the way you did? And live with that woman, and let her child—

Howard: Linda, let me tell you something—

Linda: . . . do what you did to our kids?

Howard: That I stayed with you for approximately three years after you told me you killed your mother. And you know that.

Linda: And you know that you forced me.

Howard: I forced you to do what?

Linda: You know you forced me to tell.

Howard: I would have left if you hadn't.

Linda: But that doesn't give you the right to decide everything and just say, hey, you did that, so it's all mine. You take two kids, and I'll take two kids—split the kids apart.

Howard: You know I loved you.

Linda: Shit. I don't believe that any more than that you love the kids.

Howard: I worshipped the ground you walked on.

Linda: Hum-um . . .

Howard: Until the day you told me you killed your mother, and I've never loved you again since. Now you can sue Judy Harper all you want to for alienation of affection, but I wouldn't go back to you if you were the last woman on God's green earth.

Linda: I don't want you to come back.

Howard: Why? Tell me why. You're the one that brought all this about.

Linda: Howard—

Howard: Let me finish. You destroyed a happy marriage. You're the one—not me. And I stare at those ceilings, night after night. I've just got to know. Why did you do it?

Linda: I didn't mean to. I lost my head.

Howard: What about?

Linda: She's kinda like you. When she gets mad, she just tears you apart. Tears whoever's there apart. So I took it all those years, and I took it from you. When I stayed in that marriage. You really were both a lot alike. You all demolished me—both of you.

Howard: You demolished yourself when you killed her.

Linda: I didn't mean to. I still don't think I did it. I know I started it.

Howard: Who do you think did?

Linda: I think Sam Hugh did. But that doesn't matter. I know I started it. I did.

Howard: How many times did you hit her?

Linda: Two or three.

Howard: What did you hit her with?

Linda: She had a little . . . she was . . . I guess in the den doing something . . . she had a little . . . it wasn't a hammer, but a little something like that. It was laying there on the table. Howard, I know that I did wrong, and you know I did wrong, but still, why is it that you get to play God and say "you do whatever I say"? Do you think those two children would tell you they were happy?

Howard: Honey—

Linda: You have created an intolerable situation, and you know that.

Howard: You've told me that you've been going to a doctor.

Linda: I went to a counselor. Yes, I did.

Howard: I'm aware of the fact that you killed once. How do I know you won't go berserk and kill again?

Linda. You don't.

Howard: And at night, after the divorce, I would wonder . . . Is she coming with a key to come after me, the way she did her mother? I've also wondered, would she take and go after Judy at her home?

Linda: That's ridiculous. I think the best thing for you two is gonna be when you get married and then . . . she's gonna find out a lot of things that you haven't been telling her.

Howard: Like what?

Linda: And I think you two are going to be great for each other.

Howard: What haven't I told her? What's so bad about me?

Linda: Okay. You follow whatever Howard wants. He gets up early, you get up early. You should dress a certain way, but don't spend any money at it. You keep the house as neat as a pin, and don't cook in the microwave. You ought to be able to have a conversation with any local yokel or be able to speak to the President of the United States and entertain him. Uh, let's see…should make sure everything tastes the same every time you cook. You should be nice and sweet so that everyone will like you.

Howard: What's so wrong with that?

Linda: Go to bed and get up at the time he does.

Howard: I'd be as tired as I could be.

Linda: I'm tired, too, by the time I get the kids to bed. I just don't say "go back in your room" and make them sleep in their clothes, don't take a bath, don't worry about it.

Howard: You would stay up and watch that TV for hours after me and the children went to bed.

Linda: Howard, I wasn't sleeping.

Howard: You weren't sleeping?

Linda: No, I wasn't.

Howard: Why not?

Linda: Why do you think?

Howard: You were thinking about what you did to your mother.

Linda: Yes, it was never off my mind. I worried about it constantly. You worried enough about it as it was. When the baby came, it relieved some of the pressure. But I was not doing well, even after the baby came. I couldn't . . . it was hard for me to get up in the mornings and even function.

From the backseat, Linda screamed, "Stop the tape! Please, stop the tape!" She reached for the door handle and tried to open it. She wanted to jump out and end everything.

Hicks slowed the car and pulled over.

"You can't jump out. The doors are locked from up here. We're almost to Van Buren, so try to stay calm."

Linda fell onto the car seat, the rough upholstery scratching her face as she repeatedly rolled her face back and forth against the seat.

"Oh, Jesus," she wailed, "please, help me. You know I didn't mean to. Oh, Jesus, please, please, please, help me." And then her words changed into nothing but gibberish and sobs and moans.

Linda had no idea that her ex-husband, the father of her four boys, was following behind the police car. In his car, he carried a passenger, their fourteen-year-old son.

"I want to prove to you how awful your mother is," he said. "I want you to see your mother arrested for the murder of your grandmother. How do you like that? I hope you'll never try to defend her to me again. She's a horrible, horrible person. I think she killed Parky in front of Bobby. She said he wasn't there, but I know he was."

"I don't believe it," the teenager answered. "Not Mom. Not my mom."

Howard had dropped the other three boys with a prearranged sitter. He had no intention of taking the four boys to the movie. Why, he couldn't manage four boys in a movie theatre. How ridiculous would that be? Linda was so dumb that she actually believed he would do such a thing. Oh, he was going to put her away for a long, long time. He'd get control of the boys' inheritance, and he'd be rid of Linda Park Martin forever.

Howard turned and looked at Carl.

"Stop those tears this instant. Be a man, not a little sissy like your Uncle Sam Hugh is. Like he was, I mean."

CHAPTER TWENTY-SEVEN

At the Municipal Complex in Van Buren, a crowd gathered. Newsmen and television cameramen were poised and ready. Word had spread that a suspect in the murder of Ruie Ann Park would be arriving with Chief Robertson and Assistant Chief Wayne Hicks. Deputies admonished drivers who had stopped their vehicles to move on. One deputy even pulled out his billy club to convince the driver of a white van to move along. Something big was happening, and everyone sensed it.

By the time Hicks put his car into park, Linda was crying uncontrollably. She'd seen the crowd gathered at the complex, and she tried to hide on the floorboard. All the parking lot lights were on and shone down on the people milling around.

"Get out, Mrs. Martin," the police chief said as he opened the rear door. Linda shook her head and moaned.

The chief motioned to a female officer, Charlotte Williams, who was dressed in civilian clothes, to assist Linda out of the car. Williams was young and blonde and had a sweet face.

"I've got you," she said. "Don't be afraid. I'll stay with you and help you inside." The female officer was strong and lifted Linda off the floorboard. "Try to walk."

But Linda was unable to move her feet, so she was dragged inside. She covered her face with her hands when she saw the cameras pointed at her.

"I want my baby," she wailed. "I want my boys."

When they got her inside, they took her to the camera room for pictures and fingerprinting. She wore a striped shirt, jeans, and leather dress shoes, and her black, curly hair was cut short, and it appeared to be freshly shampooed. The purse she was allowed to bring with her from Cabot was taken and stored in a locked cabinet.

The female deputy tried to help her sit down, but she just slid onto the floor. She seemed unable to control her body, and she was sobbing in harsh gulps. The policemen thought she might become hysterical and somehow injure herself. They couldn't get her to speak, and they wondered if she was even aware of where she was.

The city policemen and the county officers were elated. After three years, they'd finally caught the murderer of Ruie Park. Even though they had all been sure that Sam Hugh Park had killed his mother, they all felt a little guilty. Of course, they would never admit that their harassment had contributed to the demise of Sam Hugh Park, and it was sometime later that Assistant Police Chief Wayne Hicks went to the cemetery and poured a bottle of Jim Beam on Sam Hugh's grave. What he said at the scene, nobody knew, and, indeed, he might not have said anything. His action with the whiskey was apology enough.

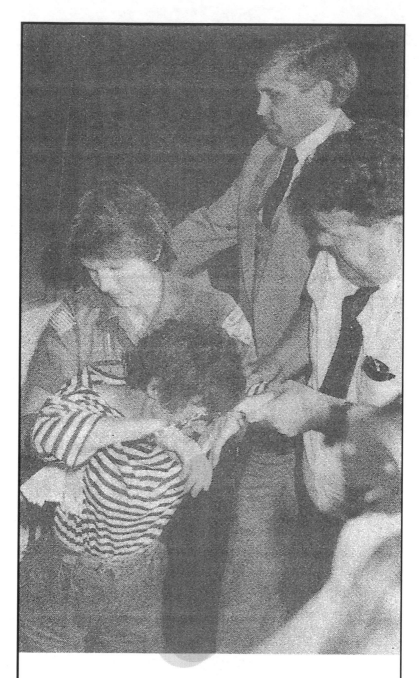

**Linda, under arrest
for murder**

CHAPTER TWENTY-EIGHT

Linda was unable to walk. Or talk. She couldn't answer questions. All she was capable of was moaning and crying. Chief Robertson was concerned, and he thought it would be wise to transfer her to Sparks Hospital in Fort Smith rather than the small hospital in Van Buren, where she might be harassed by the press and curious townspeople. There, in another town in another county, she could have a quiet place to sleep without the clamoring of the press in the municipal complex. She would also be placed on a suicide watch. He wanted to be very careful that he wasn't violating any of the rights she possessed as a person innocent until proven guilty.

He asked Hicks to take her across the river to Sparks Hospital, and she was carried into his police car by the same woman who helped get her out of the car. Hicks sped out of town south on Highway 59 and got on Interstate 540 that took him across the Arkansas River. He hoped the damned press hadn't followed him, but he took a sashay by the other hospital in town in order to throw off anyone who might be following him.

It took about fifteen minutes for him to reach the hospital in the middle of the second-largest city in Arkansas. With a rich history of lawlessness, it had been founded as a way to keep peace between the Osage and Cherokees and the settlers in the Indian Nation of Oklahoma. In its heyday, there were as many saloons and whorehouses in Fort Smith as there were churches. The infamous Federal Judge Isaac Parker and his team of deputies held court over the outlaws who committed crimes in both Arkansas and the Indian Territory.

There was still an attitude of frontier independence in Fort Smith that was looked down on by those in the capitol city of Little Rock. Furniture companies had traditionally prospered here on the backs of poorly paid employees, and the big factories like Whirlpool and Gerber Foods found that pervading attitude an exceptional arena in which to make money for themselves and their investors. There were two country clubs in town, a nice mall, and more than a few good restaurants. People in Fort Smith cheered for their high school football and basketball teams, drove the sixty miles north to Fayetteville to call the hogs at Razorback football games, and went to church. Anything that smacked of culture had a hard time surviving.

Hicks pulled into the Sparks emergency entrance and waited for someone to help him get Linda out of the car. She was still moaning and limp, and she acted as if she had no idea where she was. He opened the door when a male nurse tapped on his window.

Hicks opened his door and leaned against the car.

"I've got a prisoner I want you to keep overnight. She's out of it, and we don't want anything to happen to her before we get her arraigned tomorrow morning in Crawford County Circuit Court."

"I know. We got the call," the young man said as he rolled a wheelchair next to the back passenger door. He was tall and muscular and had long, black hair that was pulled back and secured with a rubber band. He easily lifted Linda out of the car and into the chair, and she didn't even look at him.

Hicks thanked the nurse and climbed back behind the wheel. He arched his back and rotated his shoulders two or three times. He was tired. Bone tired. All he wanted to do was get home. He drove back to Van Buren as fast as he'd driven to Fort Smith. He was eager to see his wife and get some of Wanda's cooking on a fork.

After a warmed-up supper of fried potatoes, pinto beans, and pork chops, Hicks fell into his chair in front of the television. Channel 5 News was reporting the arrest of Linda Martin for the murder of her mother. They showed him ushering her into the police station. He winced at how fat he looked. He blamed his weight gain on Wanda's home cooking. He'd have to tell her to ease up on the fried food.

When the news was over, he went into the bathroom and cleaned up a little. He was going back to the police station. He'd been demoted from chief to assistant chief by Mayor Gene Bell, who thought Van Buren needed a better trained man as chief. Gary Robertson had been a patrolman for the Arkansas State Police, scored high on some procedural classes, and had come highly recommended to the mayor, who hired him on the spot. Hicks, of course, was bitter and talked about quitting. But Van Buren was his home, and he and his family didn't want to move, so he swallowed his pride and took orders from Robertson, who was a cocky bastard and didn't really care a hoot about Van Buren. The town was simply a stepping stone to something better, Robertson had said to more than a few people.

There were still folks milling around the complex when Hicks returned. The mayor was there, as well as Trellon Ball, the sheriff. Garrick Feldman was there with his pen, frantically scribbling notes on a pad he flipped from one page to the next. Hicks watched him for a minute, amazed at how fast Feldman could write.

The sheriff signaled Hicks to come over to a quiet corner with him.

"How's Mrs. Martin doing?" he asked after he was sure no one was around who could eavesdrop.

"Oh, man," Hicks said, "she's so pitiful. I feel sorry for the woman. Everyone in town knows Ruie Ann Park had a mean streak a mile wide. I'm sure she deserved killing."

The sheriff prided himself on being a Christian man, a decent family man, and a man the people of Crawford County trusted to carry out the laws. He pondered what Hicks said and was inclined to agree with him.

"Well, Wayne, we have to follow the law. Did she mean to do it? Was it premeditated? By that I mean, did she really drive up here with a little boy in the backseat with the intent to kill her mother? I don't think so."

"You know, I kind of wish we hadn't wired Howard Martin's law office," Hicks said.

The sheriff pulled a toothpick out of his pocket and stuck it in his mouth.

"What kind of bastard turns in the mother of his children? I know I've asked that question over and over. I keep thinking about that movie, *To Kill a Mockingbird*. Did you ever see it, Wayne?

"No, I don't go to the picture shows very often."

The sheriff smiled, remembering that his daughter had begged him and Ruby to go see it with her. Ruthy had seen it once, and she wanted her parents to go with her again. They'd gone and were glad they had.

"Well, this guy," Trellon explained, "was a real bully in town, and he was killed by a real gentle man who wasn't quite right. He stuck a knife in the bully's ribs in order to save this little boy's life. The sheriff of the town said the case was closed. He said the bully must have simply fallen on his own knife."

Hicks understood what the sheriff was saying. There were a lot of wells around Crawford County that nobody even knew about. Abandoned houses with abandoned wells. The right thing to do would be to drop those tapes into a well somewhere. Yep, that would be the right thing to do, and God wouldn't think nothing about it.

CHAPTER TWENTY-NINE

After a night at Sparks Hospital, where a doctor described her as being in a high state of agitation and emotional hysteria, Linda appeared before Judge Don Langston. Clearly in a high state of agitation—and then some—she clutched a brown paper sack against her chest. A public defender, Robert Marquette, was appointed as her attorney.

Linda refused to answer any questions Judge Langston asked her, and Marquette wisely asked that she be transferred to the state hospital for a thirty-day examination. The prosecuting attorney for both Crawford and Sebastian County, Ron Fields, requested that her bond be set at $35,000. Both requests were granted by Judge Langston, and once again, Linda was loaded into a car and taken to Little Rock, to the state's mental hospital.

This time, she rode in the back of Sheriff Ball's county car, and he delivered her there in record time. Linda was aware that menstrual blood was seeping onto the backseat, but there was nothing she could do about it. She had asked for help while she was in the hospital, but a paper sack that held a small towel was the only thing provided to her. She could sense there was not much sympathy given to a woman who had killed her mother.

When she arrived at the state hospital, she stood next to a black woman named Gloria, who was being checked in. Gloria clearly didn't think she deserved to be in a nuthouse and cursed everyone in sight. As far as she was concerned, everybody could just go fuck themselves.

Linda stepped as far away from the woman as she could and looked down at the concrete floor. When she felt a tug on her arm, she looked up to see a gray-haired woman behind a metal desk.

"I need your name and birthday, ma'am."

Unlike Gloria, Linda wasn't going to give anyone any trouble. She struggled to answer questions, but finally she was able to tell the woman her name and birthday. With a clean, white gown under her arm, Linda was led into a ward of other new patients. All she could think about were her children and when she would see them again. That was the only thing that kept her from screaming, screaming, screaming.

While Linda was locked in a building with metal screens on the window, her husband was trying to get their younger children settled in. The youngest, still in diapers, required a good deal of hands-on care that Howard was unable to provide. He asked for help from Judy, the woman he now loved, to find sitters for him, and she was pleased to help. Not personally, but she would find someone who needed a job, and Cabot was full of those kind of women.

The older boys were frightened. Scared of what would happen to their mother, scared of what would happen to them. The fourteen-year-old was already ensconced in a rebellious age of disliking everyone, except his friends. But his friends had heard the news about his mother. And their parents weren't sure they wanted their teens to associate with any of the Martin kids.

CHAPTER THIRTY

Howard Martin portrayed himself around the town of Cabot as the prince who had ridden in on a white horse and valiantly put away personal feelings to further the cause of justice. Not everyone had the same opinion of him, particularly those who had taught elementary school with Linda, played bridge with her, shared homeroom responsibilities, and helped her in the concession stand at Little League ball games.

The phone lines were buzzing with the older women in Van Buren, who had seen the televised account of Assistant Chief Wayne Hicks taking Linda into the police station. They had read the newspapers in disbelief and had seen the pictures. Many well-remembered Ruie Ann Park's haughty ways, her devotion to her son, and her disinterest in her little adopted daughter.

Carmen Hampton, the wife of a Missouri Pacific railroad man, whose three sons had attended all twelve years of school in Van Buren, was particularly incensed.

"I remember when Ruie Ann first got that little girl," she told her Sunday School class at the First Baptist Church. "She showed her off in cute little dresses and bows, but everyone could see Linda was scared to death. I do believe Ruie Ann Park was the meanest woman I ever knew. And I don't doubt for one minute she deserved what she got, but Linda didn't do it."

Van Buren classmates rallied around Linda with plans to show their support. Some wanted to put up a billboard on I-540 at the Crawford County line, so when Linda's husband was driving west toward Van Buren, he would see a billboard that read: HOWARD MARTIN, STAY OUT OF CRAWFORD COUNTY. Others planned to sit together at the trial and hold up signs on the courthouse lawn.

But that was not going to happen. Howard Martin had already contacted a smart, young lawyer from Little Rock, Steve Engstrom. Martin didn't know this Bob Marquette, the public defender, and he thought his ex-wife should have someone defending her who didn't have ties to Crawford County. Howard didn't want a trial, but he did want Linda out of his life once and for all. The State Penitentiary in Pine Bluff would be a perfect place for her.

While Marquette was still on the case, and in the days following Linda's arrest, he questioned the legality of how the Van Buren Police had seemingly leaked classified information to the press, as well as to private citizens. *The Press Argus* was singled out in particular as printing information detailing the alleged evidence in the Park murder case. Marquette was quoted as saying, "The police were so excited to make the arrest and, in their exuberance, have damaged their case. Everyone here has her convicted already."

There was talk of a change of venue, or even a dismissal of charges. Ron Fields, the busy prosecuting attorney in charge of two counties, issued a statement.

"The Arkansas Supreme Court has set down guidelines concerning what is proper and improper for law enforcement agencies to release to the press. These guidelines have been furnished to Crawford County law enforcement officers on at least two occasions by our office.

"Some of the rules on pretrial publicity prohibit law enforcement agencies from discussing the identity, testimony, or credibility of prospective witnesses, or announcing the existence or contents of any confession, admission, or statements given by the accused, and deliberately posing a person in custody for photography or televising by representatives of the news media."

Van Buren Chief of Police, Gary Robertson, was out of town and could not be reached for comment. Linda Park Martin was locked up in the psychiatric hospital in Little Rock. And to her supporters, who realistically knew their signs wouldn't help, it appeared that her only hope was that the charges against her were dropped.

CHAPTER THIRTY-ONE

On July sixth, more than 20 days after Linda's June fifteenth commitment, Judge Don Langston, Circuit Judge of the Twelfth Judicial District, received the July sixth, 1984, psychiatric report on Linda. The examining psychiatrist, Roy R. Ragsdill, Jr., M.D., stated that from findings derived from historical data, medical history, physical and neurological examinations, laboratory studies, a psychological assessment by staff psychologists, and a psychiatric examination by the examining psychiatrist, the diagnosis was: No Psychiatric Diagnosis.

The psychiatrist also advised that Linda Martin appeared to be aware of the nature of the charges and the proceedings taken against her, and that she was capable of cooperating with her attorney in the preparation of her defense.

He also stated that she was ready to leave the hospital and be transported back to Van Buren by the sheriff of Crawford County.

❊ ❊ ❊ ❊ ❊

On July eleventh, Linda Martin presented herself to Judge Langston. With her was Steve Engstrom of Wilson and Engstrom Law Firm, who asked for permission to represent Linda Park. Robert Marquette, the public defender, would no longer represent her.

He also asked that a new bond be set for $50,000 with 10% being paid to Sheriff Ball or secure $15,000 in cash and sign for the remaining $35,000. In a four-page letter, Engstrom said that Mrs. Martin had never been arrested for any offense prior to this, that she was a person of fine character, and enjoyed an excellent reputation in her home town of Cabot, a close-knit community. He also stated that she was financially capable of supporting herself while awaiting trial, and that she had strong community support, including several persons of substantial stature in the community. Those friends in the community would assist Mrs. Martin in every way and secure her attendance at proper times. Since Mrs. Martin had led a stable life as an elementary school teacher, homemaker, and mother of four children, she posed no appreciable risk of nonappearance.

Judge Langston approved the motion, and Linda presented Sheriff Trellon Ball with a cashier's check for $5,000, which represented 10% of the bond already set. It was ordered that she was expected to appear on her court date of October twenty-ninth of 1984.

As Linda and her attorney left the Crawford County Court House, newspaper reporters and television cameras vied for positions. Unbeknownst to them, the couple left by way of back basement stairs, where a car waited for them.

CHAPTER THIRTY-TWO

Linda returned to her little rent house in Cabot. Her friends rallied behind her, and Linda wanted to hire Sam Sexton, a criminal lawyer, who was known to get his clients off. His office was in Fort Smith, and whenever any criminal court case was reported in the newspaper, chances were that Sexton was the attorney for the defense.

Linda also liked what she heard about Eddie Christian, a young attorney, who was quickly making a name for himself as a "go-to guy" if you needed an aggressive defense lawyer.

But Howard insisted upon Engstrom, and she simply didn't have the stamina to fight him. She wanted to tell her side of the story, and she relived the events of May sixteenth, 1981, over and over again. It still seemed like a dream, but she knew it wasn't. She had thought she would go crazy with the guilt of it, but when she'd turned up pregnant with a fourth child, she had realized she had to keep it together because of the new baby and the other boys.

Before that awful night in May, Howard had taken Carl on a weekend Boy Scout camping trip. She and Howard had argued bitterly before he left on that Friday afternoon. Linda had accused him of having an affair, and she thought he only halfheartedly denied it. The signs were there, but she didn't have absolute proof. He had told her he would be more than happy to get a divorce, but then who would take care of her.

He'd laughed and said, "Do you think your mother would let you move in with her? Not on your life, sister. You disobeyed her when you married me. Ruie Ann doesn't like anyone to disobey her. Sam Hugh can slide by, but not you."

The next morning, Saturday, Linda had awakened after a bad dream, in which she was back at the orphanage in Kansas City, watching for her natural mother to come and get her. The dream was jumbled up with a bunch of other things—Sam Hugh riding in a little cart pulled by a pony, and Sheila Jackson, her one and only real friend, who moved off to California.

It's funny how a dream can affect you. She had felt melancholy all day, and when Grandma Martin called to see if Harry, the five-year-old, could spend the night, she said okay.

"I'll feel like I'm on vacation," she told Grandma when she arrived for Harry. "I can watch whatever I want to."

But as that Saturday had worn on into evening, Linda didn't feel any happier. She'd fed the neighborhood cat that wandered by, the cat Howard forbade her to feed. On the spur of the moment, she had decided to drive to Van Buren. She packed a change of clothes for her and the baby and got in Howard's little red car, the car she wasn't supposed to ever drive because it belonged to his law firm and was written off as a tax deduction. But he'd taken the station wagon, and their other car wasn't safe to drive.

Linda had felt almost happy driving to Van Buren. She glanced in the rearview mirror and saw that Bobby was sleeping soundly. He hadn't stirred when she'd picked him up out of his baby bed and settled him in the backseat with his blanky. The night had been warm, but not warm enough to turn on the air conditioner. She'd tried driving with the windows down, but she had been afraid the wind would wake up the baby. There hadn't been much traffic past Conway, and she'd listened to the car radio on the "oldies but goodies" station. By the time she'd gotten out of range for that station, she was almost to the city limits of Van Buren. She hoped her mother wouldn't already be in bed, and she practiced what she'd tell her about Howard.

When she exited I-40 at the Van Buren exit, she headed up Highway 59. At the top of the hill, she'd turned left past the three rent houses her mother owned. Her brother lived in one of them, and the only light she saw in Sam Hugh's house came from a television in his living room. That had surprised her because he usually had parties on the weekend.

She'd left the baby in the backseat for a moment until she got her mother to open the den door. She had knocked on the glass, calling, "Mother, it's me, Linda."

Her mother, clad in her nightgown, had opened the door slightly. Her hair had been set in pin curls.

"For God's sake, Linda, what are you doing here this time of night?" she said, hissing the words.

"I just felt the need to come home, Mother."

Ruie Ann had pushed open the door and motioned for Linda to enter.

"Couldn't you have waited till morning?"

Linda had realized then that it had been a mistake to come, and she'd fought back tears. For once, she vowed, she was not going to let her mother see her cry.

"Can I come in? Just to use the bathroom?"

"Where's that gang of kids of yours?"

Linda had lowered her head and whispered, "I just brought the baby. Howard took Carl on a Boy Scout trip, and Harry is at his granny's. Bobby's asleep in the backseat."

"I'm ready for bed. Not ready for company."

"I'll just go to the bathroom, and then I'll go back home."

"And waste the gas money? You always do the craziest things. I suppose you had a fight again with Howard. I told you not to marry him. He was a gold digger. Thought we had a lot of money. Thought he'd get prestige by marrying into the Park family. Why, you're not even a real Park. You just go back to dinky little Cabot and apologize for whatever made him mad."

"Please, Mother," Linda said. "I know I should have called first. It was just a spur of the moment thing."

"Yep, that's right. Spur of the moment, that's you. I got you from that orphanage on a spur of the moment decision, and look what that got me."

Linda had gone into the guest bathroom and cupped her hands under the faucet, trying to wash away her tears. She dared not wipe her hands on the guest towels, so she'd dried them on the seat of her pants. She stayed in there longer than she should have, but she'd felt she was going to throw up. When she came out, she had walked outside to check on the baby, only to find he hadn't moved from the position she'd first lain him in. She'd walked back inside, through the den, and into the kitchen, where she thought her mother would be.

"Mother, where are you?"

"Oh, I'm back here in the guest room, fixing a bed for you and Bobby," she had called.

Linda turned and headed back through the den and down the hall to the guest room. Absentmindedly, she had picked up a wooden gavel from the coffee table. It must have come off one of Sam Hugh's plaques.

"Mother, don't fix the bed," she said. "We're not staying."

Her mother sat at the foot of the bed. "So now I don't have to make up this bed. Is that what you're telling me?"

"I told you I would leave, Mother. I'm leaving, and I'll never come back."

Ruie Ann Park had crossed her arms across her chest. "Oh, you'll try to come back, but I won't let you in the door. I'll have the keys changed. You are just a misfit. You should have never been born. You brought three stupid little boys into this world, and they'll be misfits, too."

When she heard her mother make ugly remarks about her children, Linda had exploded with rage. She'd hit her mother on her head with the gavel she held in her hand. She hit her over and over again. She lost control. She had been in a rage, a blind rage. Powerless to stop, she had kept hitting her mother until no more angry, vicious words came out of Ruie Ann Park's mouth.

For some reason, and Linda would never understand why, she had grabbed her mother's ankles and dragged her into the den. Panting and almost out of breath from exerting every bit of strength to do so, she had gone into the kitchen, moving a kitchen chair away from a window and sitting down, trying to think.

I've got to get home, she thought. *I've got to get home to Cabot. I don't have any choice. It's Howard or nothing.*

On the way home, at the Mulberry exit, she had thrown the gavel out the window. And at eleven the next morning, she had been sitting in her spot on the pew on the right side, near the back. When the preacher had asked for a moment of silent prayer, Linda had pleaded with God to forgive her.

"She just backed me into a corner, God," she had prayed, her lips barely moving. "It was just a moment of blind rage."

And then, only a few days after her mother's funeral, Howard had figured it out. He'd checked the mileage on the little red car before he left for the Boy Scout trip and checked it again when he got back. For six weeks, he had constantly quizzed her.

"Did you kill her? Tell me. Did you kill her?" He'd used the best courtroom tactics he could muster up. Finally, she had just given in and confessed.

"Don't say a word about this to anyone," he told her. "It will look bad on me. I've got my career to think about. Nobody will want to hire a lawyer whose wife killed her mother. You are never to go back to Van Buren unless I go with you. Is that understood? I don't want you getting all remorseful on me or anything."

Linda had told her husband she'd do what he said. She got up from the living room couch and went into their bedroom. He had followed, and two months later, Linda dipped a pregnancy stick into a drop of her urine, and it read positive.

CHAPTER THIRTY-THREE

The despair of having the father of her sons turn her in as a murderer equaled the despair Linda felt over killing her mother. She hadn't planned to kill her mother—it just happened. Howard had turned her in on purpose. He told the police to wire his office, and he'd get her to confess while they were having a general conversation over the reopening of their settlement agreement. Linda had even felt she made some headway with him because he seemed so genuinely pleased that she had some job interviews that might turn out okay for her. But now, after everything had come out in the wash, she knew he'd been baiting her to implicate herself while their conversation was being recorded.

Her friends in Cabot never questioned her innocence or guilt. Around bridge tables, the conversations were one hundred percent in favor of Linda.

"It's just a gut feeling I have," said one hostess of the month as she dealt the cards. The lady who brought the lemon bars for dessert agreed, and the hostess's husband, who watched a Cardinals game on TV in the den, yelled out his agreement, which caused the ladies to lower their voices and wonder what else he had heard.

But what none of her friends could understand was why Linda would let Howard tell her which lawyer to hire. Her friends didn't know what it was like to be cowed like a dog that has been beaten by his master. If she'd had a tail, Linda would have tucked it under her and sulked under a porch.

Guila refused to believe Linda was guilty. She often said, "If anyone killed that woman, it was Howard." She had no respect for Howard or his mother, and it was her misfortune to have known them long before she'd known Linda. When Linda and Howard lived in North Little Rock, his mother had told Guila that she couldn't be friends with both Linda and her.

"You know what I said to that bitch, don't you?"

The younger children were still with Linda, and they played with their Matchbox cars and Garfield toys. She saw the older boys fairly often.

The oldest was fourteen, and he seemed distant to his mom and three brothers.

"I don't want to have to hang out with my brothers, Mom. I want to be with my friends. Or just be left alone."

Linda didn't know if he was exhibiting typical teenage angst or if it was something else. During one late night discussion, he cried.

"You don't understand, Mom. I saw them carry you out of the police car."

Linda tried to embrace him. "I'm sorry your dad made you see that. He shouldn't have done that."

"Well, maybe, Mom, you shouldn't have done what you did."

She worried about what would happen to her boys. She didn't have much of the $50,000 left after her mother's and brother's estates were settled, including the sale of the White Palace. And she had to pay Engstrom for representing her so far. He told her he'd try to work out a deal, but if they had to go to trial, his fee would just about wipe out what she had left. That money, though, was frozen until the outcome of the trial. Her friends loaned her money, knowing they might never get it back.

That summer of 1984 was one of the hottest on record. Most people who could stayed indoors with their air conditioners on full blast. They sat in front of their television sets watching *Cheers* and *Dynasty*. Women got their chores done in the morning and the evening meal prepared before the kitchen got too hot to have the oven on. At Howard's house, the azaleas Linda had lovingly planted died from lack of water. So did the dogwood in the front yard.

Football season arrived, bringing people out from their summer hibernation. The residents of Cabot and Van Buren, and those of just about every other town in Arkansas, cheered for their teams. Friday night football was the cheapest and most attended spectator event throughout the state. People paid two or three bucks to get in, fifty cents for a Coke, a quarter for a Baby Ruth. Parents shelled out money so their daughters could buy cheerleading skirts and sweaters, drill team uniforms, and pep club outfits. The boys either played football or marched in the band, and everyone came to watch their kids or their neighbors' kids. Everyone came out the winner. The school profited and bought new band uniforms and new football gear. Higher salaries were offered to seemingly better coaches who had won more games, who, in turn, demanded bigger and better stadiums, equipped with weight rooms and press boxes, like those winning teams they had read about in *Sports Illustrated*.

And in the stands, the men watched the game, the women gossiped about Linda Martin, and in bed later that night, the husbands asked their wives what they had heard.

CHAPTER THIRTY-FOUR

During that month of September, when high school teams played football on Friday nights, and the Razorbacks played their games in the Southwest Conference, which was made up of Texas schools plus Arkansas, Steve Engstrom was working on Linda's case. He didn't want to go to trial, Howard didn't want to go to trial, and Linda did what she was told. Finally, the prosecuting attorney, Ron Fields, agreed to a lesser charge.

Steve Engstrom wrote Ron Fields the following letter on September nineteenth, 1984.

> *This will confirm our agreement that the State will amend the charge from murder in the first degree and, subsequent to a plea of guilty to the charge of murder in the second degree, the following sentencing options will be pursued: (1) no fine and twenty years imprisonment or (2) no fine and opportunity to appear before the Judge and argue mitigating circumstances in an effort to convince the Judge to impose less than twenty years on the second degree murder charge.*
>
> *This will also confirm that you have agreed that this is not a case where you will oppose early release on*

parole. Likewise, Linda Martin will be permitted some reasonable time to arrange her affairs (approximately thirty days) before reporting to the Arkansas Department of Corrections.

Cordially,

Stephen Engstrom

On the twenty-first day of September, Circuit Court Judge Don Langston signed the judgment that sentenced Linda Park Martin to the maximum confinement of a term of twenty years at the Arkansas Department of Corrections. Judge Langston also ruled that Linda be given thirty days credit for time served in the County Detention center. And, as a nice little surprise for the defendant, she would receive a check for $4,500 from the bond money that she had posted. Five hundred dollars would be kept out as a 10% fee to the sheriff's office.

A picture of Linda and her attorney as they were leaving the Crawford County Courthouse appeared in the Fort Smith newspaper the next day. She wore a dress with autumn colors, a jacket that came to the waist, and she had a cute, short haircut. Her lawyer was dressed in an expensive suit and wearing a pair of large, owlish glasses popular at that time. Neither Linda nor Steve Engstrom answered any questions that were asked of them by the reporters and news cameramen.

And back in Cabot, there were tears shed by Linda's supporters, and in North Little Rock, Guila Turner cried because she knew Linda was innocent, and she feared Linda would not survive a month locked up in prison.

But there were no tears shed by the father of her children. Linda was not going to be a problem for him for twenty years, and if he were a gambling man, he'd bet the only way she would leave prison would be in a casket.

CHAPTER THIRTY-FIVE

Linda had until the twenty-second of October to make plans before she moved to her new prison home. Devastated at the prospect of being locked up, she contemplated taking her own life. But she knew she couldn't do that. She had to stay alive for her children. If she was a model prisoner, and she certainly planned to be, and if she stayed healthy, she would one day—or so Judge Langston decreed—get out on parole.

But there were a lot of ifs, so she called a Cabot lawyer—not one picked out by Howard—to help her plan for her children should she die before them. She hired William Price Feland to draw up her Last Will and Testament, in which her friends, Mary Jane Rodgers or Sandy Dyson, were named as guardians of the person and property of each of her children during their minority. She also named James Russell Myers, the longtime friend of her deceased brother, and the People's Bank of Van Buren as co-trustees and co-executors.

Howard wanted her to sign over complete custody of their children to him. She would not. Perhaps that was the first time she had ever refused to do what he asked. Or anyone else.

* * * * * *

October twenty-second, 1984, dawned clear with a touch of fall in the air. Sheriff Trellon Ball was scheduled to take Linda to prison, and before he left for work, he asked Ruby to pray with him.

"Help this woman, dear Lord, this pitiful woman, who has to pay for her crime. I know she did a terrible thing, but forgive her for her sins. Keep her safe, dear Lord, because she has four boys who need her, especially the youngest one."

"Don't take this so hard," Ruby said after they had said their amens. "She killed her mother, and she has to pay."

"I know, I know," the sheriff said. "I've let this case get to me, and I shouldn't have. But I still can't believe a man would turn in his own wife."

Ruby handed her husband his jacket. "Ex-wife."

"I guess so, but still."

He tossed the jacket over his shoulder, kissed his wife on the cheek, and closed the door behind him.

Ruby watched her husband as he drove out of their driveway and down the street. *There goes a good man*, she thought and poured herself another cup of coffee.

Sheriff Ball obtained the necessary paperwork for the transfer of a female prisoner and left Van Buren around eight thirty. He stopped at McDonald's in Conway for coffee and a fish sandwich, killing several minutes before he continued on to pick up Linda at a prearranged time and place in North Little Rock.

Guila Turner had arranged for a going-away party. She invited eight people, and following a brunch of fruit cups and chicken salad, they waited with Linda for the sheriff.

When Sheriff Ball saw Linda and her friends, he parked at the far side of the building. He didn't want her friends to witness her getting into his car, so he walked around to where she stood and offered his arm. She turned for a last look at her friends, took his arm as if they were on a date, and walked to his car.

At one o'clock, he dropped her off at the prison information center in Pine Bluff and said his good-bye.

Linda later wrote in her diary: *The sheriff left me here saying they would take care of me. I sat and waited with my address book and makeup bag for a very long time. I tried not to cry.*

EPILOGUE

Linda was denied parole at her first hearing, despite the thousands of signatures that appeared on a petition given to the parole board. At that first hearing, a long-lost brother appeared and testified about their natural family and the problems the twelve children had encountered. He now lives in Sallisaw, Oklahoma. Rusty Myers also testified for her early release, assuring the board that Linda would never be a threat to society.

After serving four years of her sentence, she was released at the second parole hearing. During those four years, her children visited her at the penitentiary. Howard brought them sometimes, but rarely at the arranged times. Guila brought the boys often, giving them money to buy treats at the visiting center. Her friends in Cabot paid for ads to appear in the local newspaper wishing her four children "Merry Christmas" or "Happy Valentine's Day" from their mother.

Upon release, she worked at a McDonald's in Pine Bluff, Arkansas, and later as a clerk at a state agency.

She married again and moved to Florida, where she worked at a Wendy's Restaurant. Howard attempted to collect child support from his ex-wife and even wrote a letter to Wendy's headquarters demanding that part of her wages be sent to him.

She and her second husband had a happy marriage until his death. She visits her four sons often, and they have an abiding affection for each other. Her youngest, the one she left behind in diapers, is—and always will be—considered her baby.

Linda graciously allowed me to interview her for this book. She asked that I give her children different names because she didn't want her grandchildren to know her history.

When I finished writing this book, I no longer thought of Linda as the meek little person I knew in high school but as a damaged soul, who survived the best she could. Linda's a hell of a survivor, as her dear friend, Guila Turner, would say.

Linda, during happier times

ACKNOWLEDGMENTS

I want to first thank Kimberly and Duke of Pen-L Publishing for liking my true-crime novel enough to publish it. It's a book I'm proud of, and I will forever be grateful.

I owe a debt of gratitude to my Van Buren friends who helped me. P.D. DuVall encouraged me by saying this project would be perfect for my retirement years, and I didn't want to disappoint my friend since the second grade. Thanks also to Rusty and Linda Myers who welcomed me into their home and shared an abundance of information about the Park family, as well as giving me the scrapbook Ruie Ann Park kept, beginning with the day her son was born.

Kay Kincheloe Lynn knew both Sam Hugh and Linda, and she regaled me with her memories. She suggested the title, *Blind Rage*.

Glenda Cupples was the little girl in the polka-dotted dress who was the flower girl in Linda's wedding. She sent me pictures and her memories of living across the street from the Park home. She remembers that Linda always gave her presents for her birthday.

Joyce Patton and Nancy Baker shared their memories with me also. They felt only sorrow for Linda's childhood because they had witnessed instances where Linda was mistreated.

My dear friends and fellow writers, Doug Kelley; Marla Cantrell; and Dixie Kline each read the manuscript and offered their expert advice on making the book as good as I could get it. Pam Pearce, Clara Jane Rubarth, Julie Moncrief, Jim Martin, Tessa Freeman, Carla Ramer, Terah Curry, Beth Morsund, and Clay McKinney all contributed to the process of making me a better writer. I'll treasure their friendship always.

My darling daughter, Jennifer Paddock, read the manuscript and offered her suggestions just as I did for her three novels. Our relationship is and always has been built on a love of writing and reading.

My granddaughter, Sarah Williams, helped also by accompanying me on research trips. She, too, will publish a book one day.

The woman who taught me about books and the publishing business is Katy Boulden. I was her Wednesday Girl at Vivian's Book Shop for fifteen years, and it was in that little store, crammed with books from ceiling to floor, that I gained confidence in my writing skills. She told me to write this book, and everyone who knows Katy, knows that if she tells you to do something, you better do it. "One tough broad" was a nickname given to her by her youngest son, Ben.

Christina Scherrey, forty years my junior, is technically savvy and a brilliant whipper-snapper. Age is no barrier to our friendship filled with laughter.

I'm grateful to the Fort Smith Public Library and the Miller Branch, in particular. It was among those shelves of books that I reinvented a life for myself, and in so doing, I found friendships with my co-workers, as well as with our customers. JR Saulsberry, you still owe me a motorcycle ride.

And to my son, David X Williams and grandson, Zachary X Williams; my stepson, Brady Paddock; my sister and brother-in-law, Mary and Zeke Pratt; my niece and namesake, Anita Lynn Patton; my other three nieces, Marianne Guhman, Cathy Hancock, and Ann Paddock Kinder; my long-time friends, Eleanor Clark, Ann Byars, Betty Christian, Peggy Weidman, Carol Mason, and Mary Clark; I thank you for all your love and encouraging words, even though I know you grew tired of hearing me going on and on about my book.

And to my husband, Bea, and my big sister, Rita: I wish you were here to see this day.

ABOUT ANITA PADDOCK

Anita grew up in Van Buren, Arkansas, and attended high school with Sam Hugh and Linda Park, the children of the publishers of *The Press Argus* newspaper. In May of 1981, Mrs. Park was found murdered in her beautiful home on top of Log Town Hill. Nearly every-one, including the local and state police thought the Park son, a drunken homosexual lawyer committed the crime because he and his mother often argued about his sinful lifestyle. When Anita read about the case, she vowed to her husband, a Fort Smith attorney, that this was the book she would someday write. Some thirty-five years later, she came through on her vow with her non-fiction novel, *Blind Rage*.

Made in the USA
San Bernardino, CA
02 August 2015